THE GREAT
CHILI
PEPPER
COOKBOOK

THE GREAT
CHILI
PEPPER
COOKBOOK

CHARTWELL
BOOKS, INC.

A QUINTET BOOK

Published by Chartwell Books
A Division of Book Sales, Inc.
PO Box 7100
Edison, New Jersey 08818–7100

This edition produced for sale in the U.S.A., its territories
and dependencies only.

ISBN 0-7858-0247-9

This book was designed and produced by
Quintet Publishing Limited
6 Blundell Street
London N7 9BH

Creative Director: Richard Dewing
Designer: Fiona Roberts
Project Editor: Claire Tennant-Scull
Editor: Alison Leach
Photographer: David Armstrong
Home Economist: Gina Steer
Illustrator: Paul Collicutt

Typeset in Great Britain by
Central Southern Typesetters, Eastbourne
Manufactured in Malaysia by
C.H. Colour Scan Sdn. Bhd.
Printed by Star Standard
Industries (Pte.) Ltd, Singapore

The publishers would like to thank
Evergreen and Gorgeous, London N16
for kindly providing flowers for photography.

CONTENTS

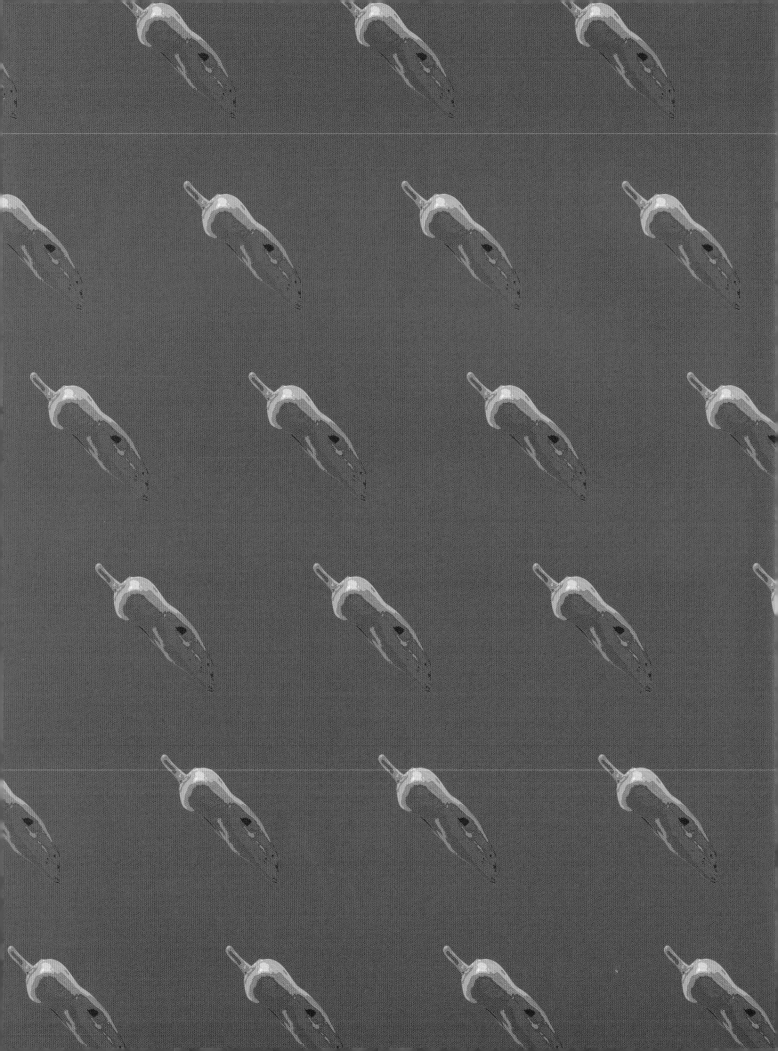

The Chili

INTRODUCTION

Traces found indicate chilies were cultivated 8–10,000 years ago. The first chilies were tiny wild berries grown in the Amazon jungle, and from their tiny seeds more than 150 varieties have evolved. They were grown in Mexico and neighboring countries, as well as in the Caribbean islands.

It was the ancestors of today's Mexicans and Indians who grew chilies, and it was the movement of the different tribes, hundreds of years ago, that brought about the vast array of varieties which are now available. The Spanish and Portuguese explorers took chilies on their travels and this resulted in chilies being grown along their trading routes to North and West Africa, Madagascar and India. They were quickly incorporated into the native cuisines. Around the middle of the 14th century, chilies reached China, the Far East and the West Indies. They even found their way to Hungary and Tibet. Today they are cultivated throughout the world, but the majority are grown in Mexico, New Mexico, California, Texas, Arizona, Louisiana, Thailand and other parts of the Far East.

Whether fresh or dried, chilies are primarily associated with Mexican and Asian cuisines. They are essential in India and Southeast Asia where much of the flavor and intensity of heat in the cooking is due to chilies. In China, too, chili is a popular seasoning, particularly in the Sichuan district, providing some very fiery dishes. One of the favorite Chinese sauces, hoisin, contains this most versatile ingredient. In the past, chilies were not used as much in the West but with the advent of more universal travel they are quickly becoming a favored ingredient.

What are chilies?

Chilies are related to the capsicum plant. They range from mild and sweet varieties to fiery hot that make the palate tingle and the eyes water. Their primary purpose has always been to flavor dishes but recent research suggests that they also have excellent medicinal qualities. They were one of the natural remedies used in ancient times as an expectorant, and for helping to prevent lung disorders, dissolve blood clots and kill pain. Today, this aspect is being explored in more detail.

The many different varieties come in assorted shapes, sizes, colors and names. Some are available only where they are grown and this often leads to great confusion, especially as even the spelling of the word "chili" varies from area to area and country to country.

Cultivation of chilies

Chilies are easy to grow in the right environment, needing only a small area and very little care and cultivation. They do best in warm, humid climates. The foliage is lush, and many varieties make attractive plants, suitable for growing in pots. The berries, which develop into the fruit or chili, have a smooth, taut skin. They are hollow, consisting of fleshy membranes or veins with many seeds. The shape varies from small elongated fruits to squat, round or even square fruit, which can be thin, flattened or plump. The colors range from green, red and orange to purple, brown and black, or even pale yellow or creamy white. Usually the smaller the chili, the hotter it is but there are always the exceptions. Remember that unripe chilies are less fiery than ripe ones. As they cross-pollinate freely, unless grown separately they will breed hybrids, which can result in a hotter chili than the original variety.

Dried chilies and chili powder

Not only are chilies available fresh, they can also be found dried, pickled and canned, as well as in chili powder, which is probably the form that most people think of when chili is mentioned. Oil flavored with chilies is now available, too, in some food stores and delicatessens. It is mainly used for marinades and stir-frying in.

Canned chilies are neither as crisp nor as fiery hot as fresh ones, whereas dried chilies can be hotter than their fresh counterparts, especially if the seeds are used as well. For heat and flavor, dried chilies and chili powder are a better substitute than canned. Drying intensifies the flavor and pungency. Good chili powder should be a deep rich color, neither too powdery nor too dry, and with a slightly lumpy consistency indicating that the natural oils have not

Red and yellow chilies hanging in a market in Hungary.

Chilies in a fruit and vegetable market in Mexico.

Uses of chilies

One of the main reasons for using chilies is for their flavor; they provide an excellent means of spicing a dish that would otherwise be bland and insipid. In tropical countries chilies are used with the same frequency that bell peppers are in the Mediterranean area and other parts of Europe. There is a widely held belief that the hotter the climate, the hotter the food. This has the effect of raising the blood temperature to that of the air temperature, thus making you feel cool. Hot, fiery food also helps the sweat glands to work, a crucial function in very hot climates.

Chilies are used in all types of savory foods, from soups, sauces, fish, meat and poultry dishes, to chutneys, pickles and dips, as well as for garnishes.

Utensils

When using either fresh or dried chilies, a mortar and pestle is an invaluable aid in the kitchen. This will enable you to pound the chilies to the correct consistency, whether a paste is required or just finely ground chilies. You can use a food processor for grinding or pounding but it is not nearly as effective. However, a food processor or blender is ideal for blending soups and sauces and forming purées.

A selection of sharp knives is essential in any kitchen, as are heavy-based pans and bowls.

How to handle chilies

Great care must be exercised when handling chilies because the oils in the chilies are an irritant to the skin. A pair of rubber gloves is a good investment, for the hotter the chili, the hotter the effect can be on your skin. Always cover any cuts on your hands when using chilies, and never rub your eyes, mouth or nose after handling chilies until you have washed your hands thoroughly. If by any chance you do get some of the chili oil on your face or in your eyes, rinse thoroughly in plenty of cold water.

Some people advocate using oil to counteract "chili burn" and milk is reputed by some to be better than water to drink.

been lost. These oils should leave a slight stain on the fingers when rubbed and the aroma should be intense. The most commonly known chili powders are cayenne and paprika. These are made from one type of chili, whereas chili seasoning is made from a variety of different chilies. There are also many different chili sauces on the market, Tabasco and the Caribbean Hot-Pepper Sauce being among the most popular and best known.

If you wish to dry your own chilies, thread different types of fresh chili together, rather like a string of onions, then hang near a sunny window and leave until completely dry before storing. Dried chilies and chili powder should be stored in airtight containers, in a cool, dark place and used within 4 to 6 months.

But whatever the name, spelling or type, one thing is sure: chilies are an invaluable food ingredient and no cook should be without these versatile fiery little spices.

Preparation of chilies

To peel fresh chilies, place under a preheated broiler and cook for a few minutes, turning frequently, until the skin has blistered and blackened. Take care, however, not to burn the flesh. You can also pierce the chili with a skewer and hold it over a gas flame to blister, or dip it quickly in hot oil. Once the chili skin has blistered, place in a bowl, cover with plastic wrap and leave the chili to cool. (You can put the chili into a plastic bag instead.) This will take about 10 minutes. Then peel, cut in half and discard the seeds and fleshy membrane, using a spoon or small sharp knife. Avoid washing chilies as you will remove the oils and impair their flavor.

Dried chilies should be roasted and rehydrated before use. Lightly roast or dry-fry the dried chilies for a few minutes, taking care not to burn them. Cover with very hot, but not boiling, water and leave to soak for about 10 minutes, until softened. Drain and use as required in the recipes. The seeds and membranes can then be easily removed and discarded.

Garnishes

Chilies can make most attractive garnishes for the dishes in which they feature. With a sharp knife or scissors, a board and a bowl of cold water, chilies can easily be transformed into flowers in about 10 minutes.

Rinse the chili lightly, then, using a small sharp knife or scissors, slit down the length of the chili almost to the stem, give the chili a slight turn and cut again. Repeat the turning and cutting until the chili has been cut all the way around. Carefully remove and discard the seeds. If any of the cuts are thick, then cut again to make finer petals. Place in a bowl of cold or iced water for 5 to 10 minutes, or until the chili has curled and formed a flower. Dry gently on paper towels.

Chopped or sliced chili can also be used as a garnish, sprinkled over the finished dish, to provide color and extra piquancy.

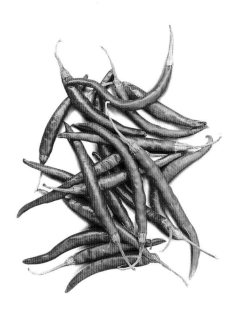

A GUIDE TO FRESH *and* DRIED CHILIES

Chilies are normally green in color before ripening and turning yellow, orange, red, purple, brown or black. They are used in both their unripened and ripened state. Green or red is often used to describe a different stage of ripeness, rather than to denote a specific variety. For instance, you can get a green fresno as well as a red fresno.

*W*hen buying fresh chilies, look for firm, shiny, dry and heavy chilies, with a fresh clean aroma; avoid those that are discolored or limp. Store, after rinsing and drying, wrapped in paper towels in the salad compartment of the refrigerator, where they will keep for 2 to 3 weeks. If chilies are kept in plastic bags, moisture will build up and spoilage will occur, and if not kept in the refrigerator, they will quickly shrivel and become limp and spoil.

Remember the heat is in the membrane or vein, not the seeds, and when a recipe calls for the chili to be seeded, the membrane needs to be removed as well. If a hotter flavor is required than the chili you are using will provide, simply leave the seeds and membrane intact. It is worth noting that everyone's heat tolerance varies, and what one person finds hot, another will not. Equally after eating chili-based dishes for a time, the palate's heat tolerance builds up and it can assimilate far hotter flavors than before.

Once you have become accustomed to chilies, it is well worth experimenting by combining two or three varieties in the same dish, thus imparting a different flavor. These, of course, can include dried and canned chilies, chili powders, seasonings and sauces.

Ají – Heat 7–8 *Thin-fleshed, tapering to a point, 3 to 5 inches in length with a tropical fruit flavor and a fierce heat. Yellow, green or red in color. Originating from Peru and other regions of South America. Ideal for salsas, sauces and pickling.*

Ají dulce – Heat 7–8 *Similar shape to a small, elongated bell pepper, 2 to 3 inches in length with a fruity but hot flavor. From bright green to orange and red. Related to the Scotch bonnet and habanero. Grown in Venezuela and north-east South America. Ideal for salsas and stews.*

Amatista – Heat 7 *Wide at the stem, tapering to a point with a rounded end, ½ to 1½ inches in length. Bright purple with an earthy, sweet flavor. Grown in South America. Ideal for pickling and garnishes.*

Anaheim – Heat 2–3 *Also known as the Californian, New Mexican or long green (or red) chili. About 6 inches in length and 2 inches in width. Either bright green or, when ripe, red. Thicker flesh than many, similar to the bell pepper with a vegetable flavor. The red Anaheim is sweeter than the green. The flavor can be improved by roasting. Grown in California, and southwest United States. Dried powdered red New Mexican chilies are sold as chili Colorado. Ideal stuffed, or for sauces and stews.*

Banana chili – Heat 2–3 *About 6 inches in length, pale green to light orange. Having a sweet flavor similar to a bell pepper with a thick flesh. The inside of the flesh is often rubbed with chili powder to impart a stronger flavor. Grown in southwest United States. Ideal for stuffing and salads.*

Chawa – Heat 3–4 *Usually curved and tapering to a point, 3 to 5 inches in length. Pale yellow with a thin flesh, having a sweet flavor with a hint of heat. Similar in appearance to the banana chili. Grown on the coast of Mexico. Ideal for salads, stuffing and pickling.*

Chili negro – Heat 3–4 Also known as chilaca, 6 to 9 inches in length, and can be curved. Dark brown to almost black. Difficult to find fresh outside Mexico but any other chili with similar heat properties or chili powder can be substituted. The dried chili negro is often called chili pasilla. Grown in Mexico and parts of South America. Ideal for pickling and sauces.

Congo – Heat 8 A small, green, very hot chili which turns red on ripening, ¼ to ½ inch in length. Grown in the Congo, Mombasa and Zanzibar.

De agua – Heat 4–5 About 4½ inches in length, tapering to a point, and either green or red, both having a vegetable flavor similar to unripe tomatoes with a thin flesh. The red has a slightly sweeter flavor. Grown in South America. Ideal for soups, mole sauces and stuffing.

Dutch – Heat 6 Also known as Holland chili, about 4 inches in length, slightly curved and bright red. Having a hot sweet flavor with a thick flesh. The Thai chili or red fresno can be substituted. Grown in the Netherlands. Ideal for soups, casseroles, sauces and pickling.

Ethiopian – Heat 2 A small chili about ¼ to ½ inch in length. A smooth mild red chili that is grown in Ethiopia and surrounding countries.

Fiesta – Heat 6–8 Ornamental chilies about 1 to 2 inches in length. Related to the cayenne and Tabasco chili, slightly tapered with a rounded end. Varying in flavor and heat from mild to hot and in color from yellow through to red. Excellent plants for pot-growing. Grown in northern Mexico and Louisiana. Ideal for garnishes, salsas and stir-fries.

Fresno – Heat 6–7 Either green or red, about 2 inches in length, full and plump, tapering to a round end. Has a thick flesh and is sweet and hot. Grown mainly in Mexico and California. Ideal for salsas, stuffing and sauces.

Güero – Heat 4–6 The generic name for any pale yellow or green chili, can also be called blond. Can vary in size from 3 to 5 inches. Has a slightly sweet flavor with a sharp tang. Heat ranges from medium to hot. Grown in northern Mexico and the southwest United States. Ideal for yellow mole sauces and garnishes.

Guntur – Heat 5 A deep red chili with a compressed base ½ to 1 inch in length. Grown in India.

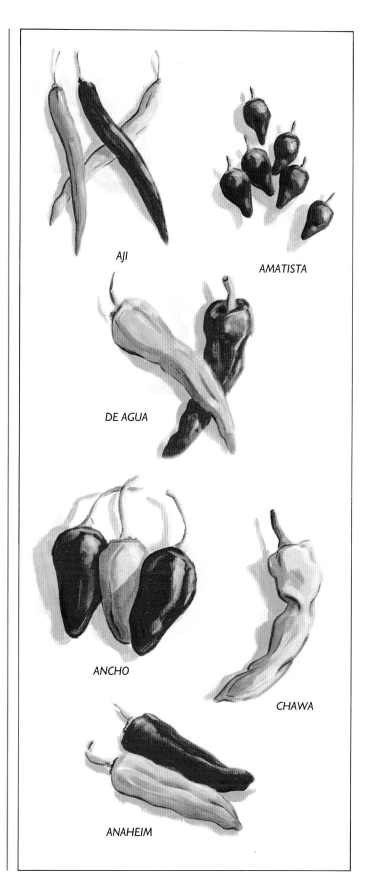

AJI

AMATISTA

DE AGUA

ANCHO

CHAWA

ANAHEIM

Habanero – Heat 10 *About 2 inches in length with a lantern shape. Varying from green and yellow to red and reddish-purple. The ripe habanero is sweet with a tropical fruity flavor. It is one of the hottest chilies available and is closely related to the Scotch bonnet and the Jamaican hot chilies. Grown in Central America and the Caribbean. Ideal in salsas, marinades, chutneys and bottled sauces.*

Honka or Hontaka – Heat 9 *From ¼ to 3 inches in length, an orange or red chili which is wrinkled in appearance. Grown in Japan.*

Huachinango – Heat 5–6 *About 4½ inches in length, tapered with a rounded end. Bright red with white or pale markings on the skin. Thick-fleshed with a sweet flavor. Often smoked and dried and used to make* chipotle grande. *Grown in central Mexico. Ideal for salsas, casseroles and sauces.*

Hungarian cherry pepper – Heat 1–3 *Round chili about 1½ inches in diameter. Bright red with plump flesh and masses of seeds. Sweet in flavor and fairly mild in heat. Grown in Hungary, Europe and California. Ideal for salads.*

Hungarian sweet chili – Heat 0–1 *About 6 inches in length, being broad at the stem with a rounded end. Bright red, mild in heat with a thick flesh, very similar to the bell pepper when used as pimientos. Grown in Hungary, Europe and California. Ideal for any dish where heat is not a requirement.*

Jalapeño – Heat 5–6 *The most commonly used chili, 2 to 3 inches in length, tapering to a rounded end. Either green or, when ripe, yellow or red, all having plump thick flesh and being very fat and juicy. When dried and smoked, known as chipotles. Varying in flavor according to the color; the green have a distinctive vegetable flavor, whereas the ripe chilies are slightly sweeter. Grown in Mexico, Texas and the southwest of the United States. Ideal for everything: salsas, soups, casseroles, sauces, dips, stuffings or pickles.*

Jamaican hot – Heat 9 *About 2 inches in length, bright red and of similar shape to the Scotch bonnet or habanero, to which they are related. Thin flesh with a sweet, hot flavor. Grown in Jamaica and other Caribbean islands. Ideal for curries, fish stews and chutneys.*

Kalyanpur, Kesanakurru and Kovilpatti – Heat varies *All Indian chilies that are used extensively throughout the country. Green and red.*

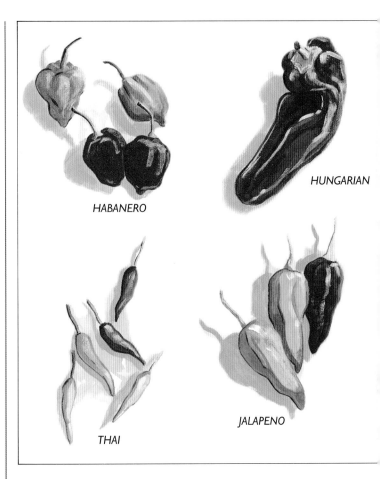

HABANERO

HUNGARIAN

THAI

JALAPENO

Kashmir – Heat 6–8 *Close relation to the jalapeño and serrano chilies, being green or red, about 1 to 2 inches in length. Also called sriracha or siracha. A sauce is made from these chilies in Thailand and sold around the world as an accompaniment to fish.*

Kenyan – Heat 2–3 *About 1 to 2 inches in length and similar in appearance to the jalapeño chili. Bright green, turning red when ripe. Grown in Kenya and surrounding countries.*

Korean – Heat 6–7 *About 3 to 4 inches in length, thin and slightly curved, tapering to a point. Bright green, thin-fleshed with a hot vegetable flavor. Related to the Thai or bird's eye chili. Grown in Korea, Japan and California. Ideal for stir-fries, marinades and pickling.*

Macho – Heat 9–10 *Tiny chilies about ¼ inch in length. Both green or red. Have a sharp, intense flavor and are very hot. Related to the pequín. Grown in South America and Mexico. Ideal for salsas and casseroles.*

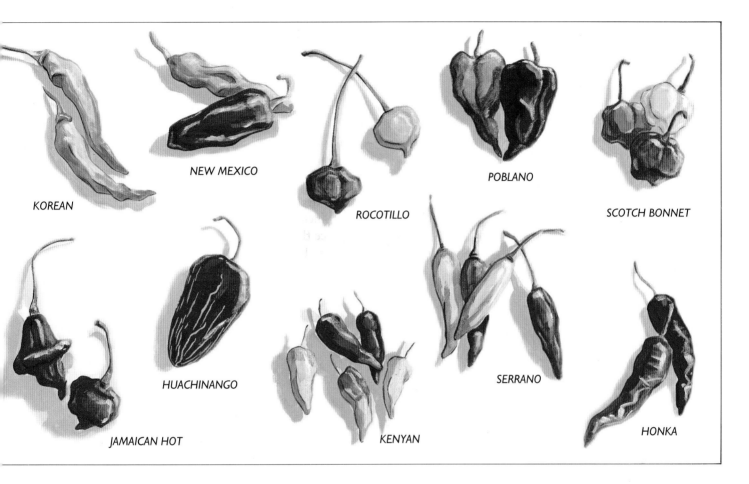

KOREAN

NEW MEXICO

ROCOTILLO

POBLANO

SCOTCH BONNET

HUACHINANGO

JAMAICAN HOT

KENYAN

SERRANO

HONKA

Manzana – Heat 6–8 Also known as chili rocoto, about 3 inches in length and is like a misshapen bell pepper. Usually yellow or orange with a thick flesh and black seeds. Has a fruity, hot flavor. Grown in Central America and Mexico. Ideal for sauces, stuffing or serving as a vegetable.

Mundu – Heat 2 A deep red short and stout chili originating in India. It is very mild in heat.

New Mexico – Heat 3–4 Both green and red, 6 to 9 inches in length. An elongated chili that varies considerably in heat, having a clear defined chili flavor. The red variety is fleshy, as is the green, but is far sweeter and known in Mexico as chili pasado when roasted and dried. These chilies freeze exceptionally well. Grown in New Mexico. Ideal for salsas, sauces, stuffing and casseroles; the red chilies are also used in red chili and barbecue sauces.

Nigerian – Heat 8–9 About ⅜ to 1¼ inches in length with a wrinkled red skin. Grown in Africa.

Peruvian – Heat 7–8 About 2 inches in length, like a very small bell pepper in shape. Green, yellow or red. Has a thin flesh with a tropical fruity flavor. Fairly intense in heat. Grown in South America. Ideal for cebiche and salsas.

Peter pepper – Heat 7 About 4 inches in length, quite a rare chili and often grown for its ornamental qualities, being very crinkled in appearance and bright red. Has a sweet, hot flavor. Grown in Louisiana and Texas. Ideal for salsas, garnishes and as an ornamental house plant.

Poblano – Heat 3 Green or red, 4 to 5 inches in length. Thick-fleshed with a medium to hot heat. The green poblano is always cooked prior to eating, and roasting gives both green and red a full earthy flavor. When dried, referred to as ancho and sometimes as pasilla, which is, in fact, incorrect. Grown in central Mexico and California. Ideal for sauces, stuffing, stews and tamales.

Prik Chee Fa – Heat 5–8 A very popular Thai chili, "prik" being the Thai name for chili. A red chili about 4 inches in length and fat in shape.

Rocotillo – *Heat 7 About 1 inch in length and squat in shape. Related to the Scotch bonnet and habanero. Because of its shape it is referred to as squash chili as it looks similar to a pattypan. Thin-fleshed with a mild fruit flavor but intense heat. Grown in South America. Ideal for pickling, salsas and sauces.*

Santa Fe Grande – *Heat 6 About 2½ inches in length. Pale yellow. Thick-fleshed with a light, fruity flavor similar to a melon. A type of güero chili. Medium to hot. Grown in north Mexico and southwest United States. Ideal for salsas, pickles and sauces.*

Santaka – *Heat 9 A very straight, thin, deep red chili. Grown in Japan.*

Scotch Bonnet – *Heat 9–10 About 1 inch in length, like a squashed Chinese lantern in shape. Pale yellow, green, orange or red with an extremely hot, fruity, yet smoky, flavor. Related to the habanero and Jamaican hot. Grown in Jamaica and other islands of the Caribbean. Ideal for jerk sauces, condiment sauces and Caribbean curries.*

Serrano – *Heat 7 About 2 inches in length, smooth with a tapered round end. A thin red or green chili with a clean, biting taste. It has a relatively high heat content, but the ripe red serrano is slightly sweeter than its green counterpart. Can be substituted for the Thai or bird's eye chili in the ratio of 3 serrano chilies to 1 Thai chili. Grown in Mexico and the southwest United States. Ideal for guacamole, stir-fries and salsas.*

Tabasco – *Heat 9 About 1 inch in length, thin-fleshed with a strong, biting heat. Bright orange or red and used mainly for making the famous Tabasco sauce. Grown in Louisiana and Central and South America.*

Tepín – *Heat 8 About ¼ inch in length, bright orange to red similar in appearance to little chilies and closely related to the wild chilies found in Mexico. Has a fiery heat that is not long-lasting. Grown in South America and desert areas. Ideal for soups and casseroles.*

Thai or Bird's Eye – *Heat 7–8 About 1½ inches in length, thin elongated with a pointed end. Thin-fleshed with many seeds and has a fierce heat. Green or red. Grown in Thailand, Asia and California. Ideal for stir-fries and all Asian dishes.*

Usimulagu – *Heat 5–8 A chili similar in shape to the Thai bird's eye but not as red and slightly milder. Grown in India.*

Dried Chilies

Like wine, dried chilies have many different flavors and it takes a connoisseur to detect the subtle differences. They vary from rich smoky and woody flavors to fruity flavors of cherries, plums or damsons, those that have a distinct citrus flavor and even some with a chocolate, licorice or coffee flavor. It takes time to develop the palate by learning about the different flavors, but it is time well spent. Chilies can transport an ordinary dish to new culinary heights, as their depth and richness in flavor is incomparable.

The drying process intensifies the flavor and gives it a real punch. On drying, the natural sugars concentrate and produce the great depth of flavors that are present.

When buying dried chilies, check that they have no discoloration or spots and are clean, not dirty or dusty. If the chili is split, much of its oil will have been lost, resulting in an inferior taste. Store in an airtight container for 3 to 4 months, certainly no longer than 6 months.

Some people recommend seeding the chili before roasting and rehydrating, while others do not; obviously the choice is up to the individual. First, lightly roast or dry-fry in a nonstick skillet for a few minutes, being careful not to burn or scorch the chili, otherwise it will taste burnt. Then cover with very hot, but never boiling, water and leave for at least 10 minutes, or until soft. Drain and then use as described in the recipe. Whether or not you discard the seeds and membrane is a personal choice, but remember the heat is in the membrane, not the seeds.

As with fresh chilies, there are many different varieties of dried chilies and if one is not available, another, or even chili powder, can be substituted. If powder is used, the flavor will, however, not be as good. Any fresh chili can be dried but the more obscure varieties are difficult to find other than in their country of origin. Below is a list of the types more commonly available in high-quality food stores or specialist shops.

Types of dried chilies

If a particular type of chili is specified in a recipe and is unobtainable, either substitute one of the equivalent heat or use more chilies with a lower heat content.

Ancho – *Heat 3–5 The dried poblano chili and one of the most commonly available. It has ripened to a deep reddish brown with a wrinkled skin. Not to be confused with the mulato, which has a blackish tinge to the skin and is not as sharp or fruity as the ancho. About 5 inches in length, having a sweet fruit flavor with hints of raisin, coffee and licorice. The ancho, mulato and pasilla form the holy trinity of chilies, and are used to make the* traditional Mexican mole sauces. Grown in Mexico and California.

Cayenne – Heat 8 About 2 to 4 inches in length, bright red with a thin body tapering to a point. Can be used in sauces and soups and is extensively used in powdered form as seasoning. Grown in Louisiana and Mexico.

Chipotle – Heat 6 A large dried smoked jalapeño, dull tan to coffee brown, about 2 to 4 inches in length. Often available in cans or jars, these are hot and normally used with their seeds and membranes intact. The chipotle grande is a dried huachinango chili which is similar in flavor but larger in size. Grown in South America and Texas.

Guajillo – Heat 2–4 One of the most-common dried chilies available, about 4 to 6 inches in length with a rough maroon skin. It has a slightly bitter or tannin flavor and the skin is often discarded after rehydration due to its toughness. Grown in north and central Mexico.

Mulato – Heat 3 About 5 inches in length, a deep dark brown chili which is round at the stem, tapering to a point. It has a smokier flavor than the ancho and the predominant taste is licorice with a hint of tobacco and cherry. Like the ancho, it is sold in Mexico in three different grades, varying in depth or taste and quality. Grown in central Mexico.

New Mexico – Heat 2–3 Like the fresh ones, these come in different colors, from olive green (from the green New Mexico chili) to bright scarlet. Being the same length as their fresh counterparts, they have all the same qualities, except the flavor is intensified. They can also be referred to as dried California chili. Often sold as crushed chili flakes. Grown in New Mexico and Rio Grande.

Pasilla – Heat 4 Also known as the chili negro, and constitutes the third member of the trinity of chilies required for a traditional mole sauce. About 6 inches in length, dark raisin brown to black, shiny and wrinkled. Pasillas range in heat from mild to fairly hot with a hint of grape and licorice. Apart from being used in mole sauces, the pasilla is also good for many other sauces and blends well with seafood dishes. Can be found in some areas as a powder. Grown in Central Mexico.

> Remember when handling chilies, great care must be exercised. If necessary, use rubber gloves. Wash fresh chilies after seeding under cold running water and in no circumstances rub your eyes, mouth or nose before you wash your hands.

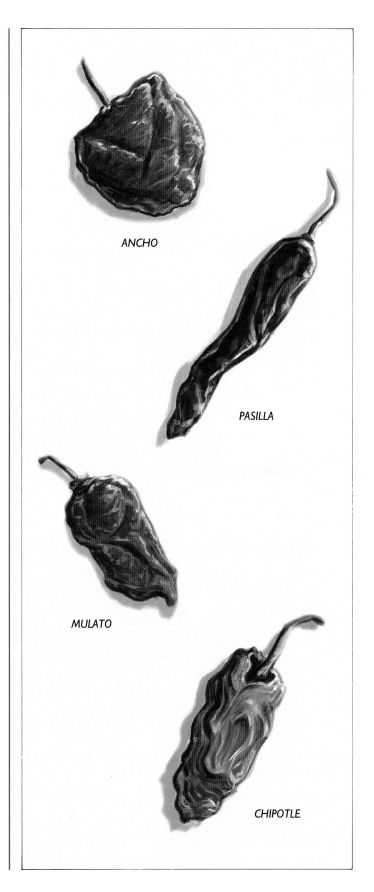

ANCHO

PASILLA

MULATO

CHIPOTLE

Chapter 1

Soups

RED PEPPER SOUP

HEAT 1

Serves 4

2 Hungarian cherry peppers
   (or red bell peppers)
2 tbsp sunflower oil
I onion, finely chopped
I garlic clove, crushed
2½ cups vegetable or chicken stock
8 oz ripe tomatoes, peeled and
   seeded
salt and pepper
2 tbsp light cream, and chopped
   Hungarian cherry pepper, to serve

🌶 Preheat the broiler. Rinse the peppers and cut in half, discarding the seeds. Place, skin-side uppermost, on a sheet of foil in a broiler pan under the broiler. Drizzle with 1 tbsp of the oil and broil for 5 to 10 minutes, or until the skins have blistered. Remove from the heat and leave to cool. When cool, remove the skins and roughly chop.

🌶 Meanwhile, heat the remaining oil in a pan and sauté the onion and garlic for 5 minutes, or until transparent but not browned. Add the chopped peppers and then the stock. Roughly chop the tomatoes and add to the pan with seasoning to taste. Bring to a boil, then cover and simmer gently for 15 minutes, or until the peppers are really soft.

🌶 Leave to cool, then purée in a food processor or strainer. If the soup is to be served hot, return to the rinsed pan, check the seasoning and reheat gently. If it is to be served cold, chill for at least 1 hour.

🌶 To serve, add the cream and swirl lightly, then sprinkle with a little chopped chili pepper.

BLACK BEAN SOUP

HEAT 5

Serves 4

1⅓ cups dried black beans
I tbsp sunflower oil
4 oz streaky back bacon, chopped
I large onion, chopped
I garlic clove, crushed
2 or 3 green jalapeño chilies,
   seeded and chopped
2 tomatoes, peeled and chopped
2½ cups vegetable or chicken stock
few sprigs of fresh cilantro
salt and pepper
freshly chopped cilantro, to garnish

Sopa de frijoles

This soup is sometimes called Poor Man's Soup. Any beans of your choice can be used.

🌶 Cover the dried black beans with cold water and soak overnight. Next day, drain, put into a large pan, cover with cold water and bring to a boil. Boil rapidly for 15 minutes, then drain and reserve.

🌶 Heat the oil in a large pan and sauté the bacon, onion, garlic and chilies for 5 minutes, stirring occasionally. Add the black beans, tomatoes and stock, and bring to a boil.

🌶 Reduce the heat to a gentle simmer. Add the sprigs of cilantro with seasoning to taste and simmer for 1 hour, or until the beans are tender and a thick consistency is reached. Remove the cilantro, check the seasoning and serve sprinkled with chopped cilantro as a garnish.

TORTILLA SOUP

HEAT 4–5

Serves 4

I tbsp corn oil
I large onion, chopped
2 to 3 fresno chilies, seeded and
   chopped
2 carrots, cut into julienne strips
3 cups vegetable or chicken stock
grated peel and juice of 2 limes
2 zucchini, trimmed and thinly sliced
salt and pepper
taco crisps
freshly chopped cilantro and sliced
   chili, to garnish

Sopa de tortilla

🌶 Heat the oil in a large pan and sauté the onion and chilies for 5 minutes, or until soft. Add the carrots with the stock and lime peel and juice. Bring to a boil. Reduce the heat, cover and simmer gently for 5 minutes.

🌶 Cut the zucchini into half-moon shapes and add to the pan with seasoning to taste. Cook for a further 3 to 5 minutes, or until the vegetables are tender. Check the seasoning.

🌶 Place a few taco crisps in the bottom of 4 individual soup bowls. Ladle the soup over and serve immediately, garnished with chopped cilantro and sliced chili.

Red Pepper Soup ▶

COLD AVOCADO SOUP

Sopa de aguacate

HEAT 2

Serves 4 to 6

1 or 2 green Anaheim chilies

1 tbsp oil

3 large ripe avocados

⅔ cup chicken or vegetable stock

1¼ cups light cream

⅔ cup milk

1 to 2 tbsp lime juice

salt and white pepper

*freshly snipped chives and sour
cream, to garnish*

Preheat the broiler to high. Cut the chilies in half and discard the seeds. Place in a broiler pan, skin-side uppermost, and drizzle with the oil. Broil for 5 minutes, or until the skin has blistered. Remove from the heat and leave to cool.

Discard the skin and membrane from the chilies and roughly chop. Put into a food processor. Peel and seed the avocados, then roughly chop and put into the processor with the stock. Blend to form a smooth purée.

With the machine still running at low speed, add the cream, then the milk.

Stir in the lime juice and seasoning to taste. Pour into a soup tureen and chill for at least 1 hour. Serve garnished with snipped chives and sour cream.

CHICKEN *and* CHILI SOUP

HEAT 8

Serves 4 to 6

1 tsp oil

1 tsp green curry paste

2½ cups chicken stock

⅔ cup coconut milk

1 or 2 bird's eye (Thai) chilies, seeded and chopped

2 lemongrass stalks, outer leaves removed and finely chopped

4 kaffir lime leaves

1-inch piece gingerroot, peeled and finely grated

12 oz chicken breasts, skinned and cut into thin strips

1 cup green beans trimmed and cut into short pieces

3-inch piece cucumber, peeled if preferred and cut into strips

½ cup cooked fragrant rice

1 to 2 tsp honey

4 tbsp light cream (optional)

➹ Heat the oil in a large pan and fry the curry paste gently for 3 minutes, stirring occasionally.

➹ Add the stock with the coconut milk, chilies, lemongrass, lime leaves and ginger. Bring to a boil and boil for 3 minutes. Reduce the heat, then add the chicken strips and simmer for 5 to 10 minutes, or until the chicken is cooked.

➹ Add the green beans and cucumber with the rice and honey. Simmer for a further 5 minutes, or until the vegetables are tender.

➹ Stir in the cream, if using, and serve.

HOT-*and*-SOUR SHRIMP SOUP

HEAT 9

Serves 4 to 6

3¾ cups fish or chicken stock

2 lemongrass stalks

1-inch piece gingerroot, peeled and
    grated

2 or 3 bird's eye (Thai) chilies, seeded
    and chopped

few fresh kaffir lime leaves

1 large carrot, cut into julienne strips

1 lb raw large shrimp, shelled and
    deveined

1½ cups wiped and sliced shiitake
    mushrooms

2 tbsp lime juice

1 tbsp Thai fish sauce

1 tsp chili paste

1 cup bean sprouts

2 tbsp freshly chopped cilantro

*This is a very fragrant soup from Thailand.
Some recipes use tamarind to give the sour
taste, others, like this one, use lime juice.*

❧ Put the stock into a large pan. Remove the outer leaves from the lemongrass and finely chop. Add to the stock with the ginger, chilies and lime leaves. Bring to a boil, then simmer for 10 minutes.

❧ Add the carrot, shrimp and mushrooms to the pan. Simmer for a further 5 to 8 minutes, or until the shrimp have turned pink.

❧ Mix the lime juice, fish sauce and chili paste together, then stir into the pan and continue simmering for 1 to 2 minutes. Add the bean sprouts and chopped cilantro, stir once and then serve.

FISH SOUP *with* CHILIES

Sinigang na isda

HEAT 4–5

Serves 4

1 tbsp oil

1 large onion, finely chopped

1 garlic clove, crushed

2 celery stalks, trimmed and chopped

2 de agua chilies, seeded and
    chopped

1½ cups peeled, seeded and chopped
    tomatoes

1 tbsp tomato paste

2 cups fish stock

1 lb white fish fillets, skinned
    and cut into bite-sized pieces

salt and pepper

flat-leaf parsley, to garnish

❧ Heat the oil in a large pan and sauté the onion, garlic, celery and chilies for 5 minutes, or until softened. Add the chopped tomatoes and tomato paste, and sauté for a further 3 minutes.

❧ Pour in the stock and bring to a boil. Reduce the heat and simmer gently for 10 minutes.

❧ Add the fish and simmer for a further 5 minutes, or until the fish is cooked. Season to taste and serve garnished with flat-leaf parsley.

Hot-and-Sour Shrimp Soup ▶

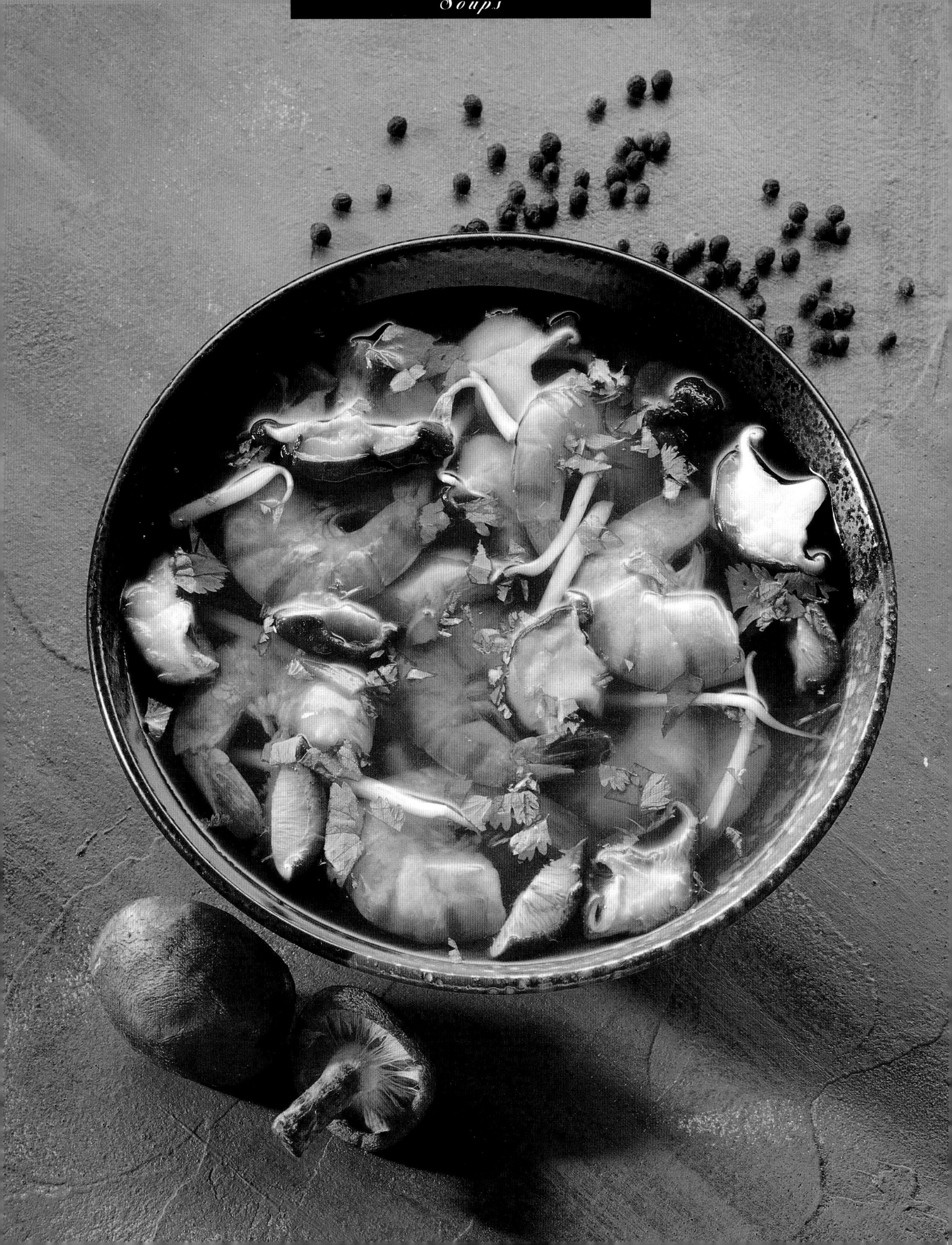

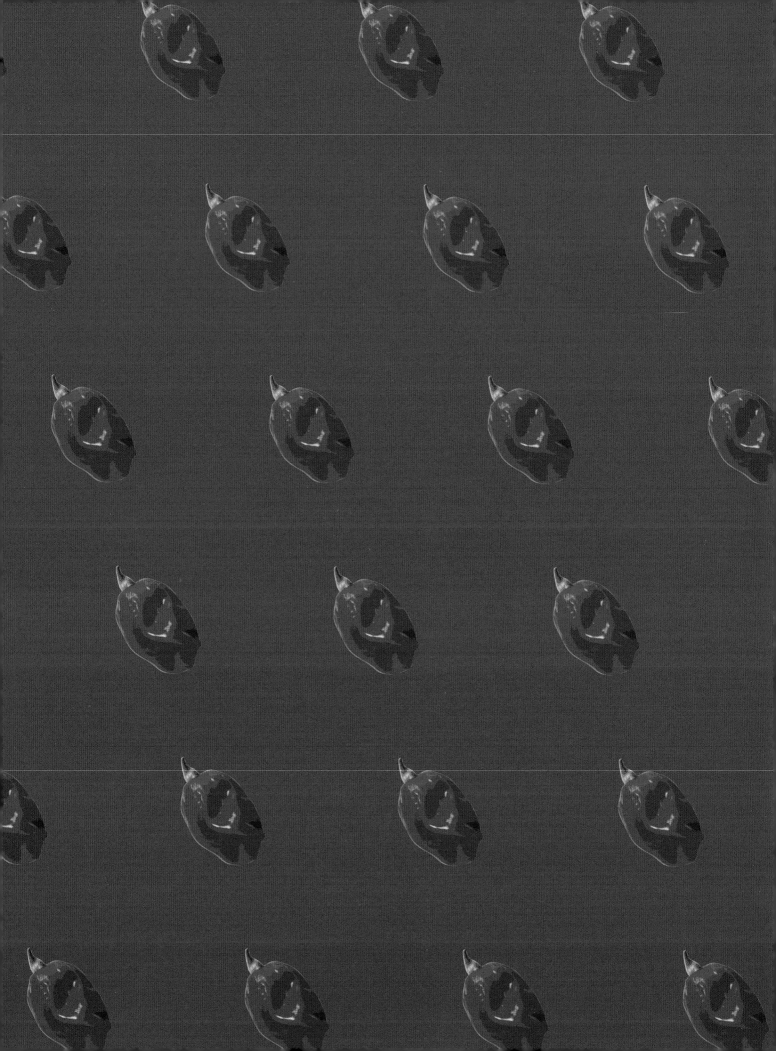

Chapter 2

Appetizers and
Salads

BEAN DIP *with* CHILI

HEAT 4–5

Serves 6 to 8

3 or 4 jalapeño chilies

2 tsp corn or olive oil

1⅓ cups drained and rinsed canned
*   red kidney beans*

1⅓ cups drained and rinsed canned
*   cannellini beans*

1 or 2 garlic cloves, crushed

4 to 5 tbsp tomato juice

1 ripe mango, peeled and sliced

1 tbsp freshly chopped oregano

extra freshly chopped oregano,
*   to garnish*

crudités, to serve

Preheat the broiler to high. Place the chilies in a broiler pan and drizzle with the oil. Broil for 4 to 5 minutes, or until the skins have blistered and blackened.

Put the chilies into a plastic bag and leave to sweat for 10 minutes; then discard the skin and seeds if a milder dip is required. Put into a food processor with the remaining ingredients and blend to form a thick dipping consistency.

Pour into a serving dish, cover and chill for 30 minutes to allow the flavors to develop. Serve, sprinkled with chopped oregano, and with the crudités.

REFRIED BEANS

Frijoles refritos

HEAT 4–5

Serves 6

1⅓ cups dried pinto or borlotti beans

3¾ cups beef or chicken stock

1 large onion, chopped

2 garlic cloves, crushed

4 green New Mexico chilies, seeded
*   and chopped*

1 tsp salt

black pepper

¼ cup lard or 3 to 4 tbsp corn
*   or olive oil*

2 tbsp sour cream (optional)

2 tbsp freshly chopped cilantro
*   or parsley*

Refried beans can also be made with red kidney beans. This is a traditional Mexican dish, but they can also be found in Spain, where "refritos" means thoroughly.

Cover the beans with cold water and leave to soak overnight. Next day, rinse and put into a saucepan. Cover with cold water and bring to a boil. Boil rapidly for 15 minutes. Drain again and return the beans to the rinsed pan.

Add the stock, onion, garlic and chilies, and bring to a boil. Reduce the heat and simmer for 1 hour, or until the beans are tender. Drain, reserving the cooking liquid.

Add the salt and pepper to the beans and mash with 4 to 5 tbsp of the cooking liquid. Alternatively, put into a food processor with the reserved cooking liquid and blend to form a chunky purée.

Heat the lard or oil in a skillet and add the mashed beans. Cook for 10 to 15 minutes, or until dry, stirring frequently, to prevent the beans sticking. Stir in the sour cream, if using, and chopped cilantro or parsley.

GUACAMOLE

HEAT 5–6

Serves 4

2 ripe avocados

1½ cups peeled, seeded and finely
 chopped ripe tomatoes

1 bunch scallions, trimmed and
 finely chopped

2 serrano chilis, seeded and finely
 chopped

1 or 2 jalapeño chilies, seeded and
 finely chopped

2 tbsp lime juice

1½ tbsp freshly chopped cilantro

salt and pepper

shredded lime peel, to garnish

taco crisps and crudités, to serve

*A very traditional Mexican dish, with many
different versions. Mexicans will serve
Guacamole as an appetizer, side
accompaniment, salad or with drinks.*

Peel the avocados and discard the seeds.
Mash the flesh with a potato masher or fork.

Add the finely chopped tomato and
scallions with the chilies and mix together well.
Stir in the lime juice with the cilantro and
seasoning to taste. Turn into a serving bowl
and fork the top.

Sprinkle with the lime peel just before
serving with taco crisps and crudités. It is best
eaten immediately but if it has to be kept, place
one of the avocado seeds in the middle, cover
and chill for no longer than 1 hour.

THAI LETTUCE PACKAGES

HEAT 7–8

Serves 4

Dipping Sauce

2 tbsp Thai fish sauce
2 garlic cloves, crushed
1 to 2 tbsp sugar
2 tbsp lime juice
2 tbsp white-wine vinegar
1 bird's eye (Thai) chili, seeded and finely chopped

Packages

1 tbsp corn or sunflower oil
1 garlic clove, crushed
2 lemongrass stalks, outer leaves removed and finely chopped
1-inch piece gingerroot, peeled and grated
2 to 3 bird's eye (Thai) red chilies, seeded and chopped
8 oz chicken breast, skinned and shredded (about 1½ cups)
1 tbsp soy sauce
2 tsp Thai fish sauce
1 cup bean sprouts
1 small iceburg lettuce, rinsed and separated into leaves

Mix all the ingredients for the sauce together and leave for at least 30 minutes for the flavors to develop.

Heat the oil in a wok or large saucepan and stir-fry the garlic, lemongrass, ginger and chilies for 2 minutes.

Add the chicken and continue to stir-fry for 5 minutes, or until the chicken is cooked.

Add the soy and fish sauce, stir once, then add the bean sprouts and stir-fry for a further 30 seconds.

Arrange spoonfuls of the chicken mixture on a lettuce leaf and drizzle with a little of the sauce. Roll up to form a package and serve.

PICKLED SPICY VEGETABLES

HEAT 6–7

Makes 3 x 2-lb jars

8 oz eggplant
1½ cups sliced carrots
8 oz pear onions
8 oz beans, trimmed and sliced in half if large
1 red bell pepper, seeded and sliced
1 green bell pepper, seeded and sliced
2 tbsp salt
3 to 4 Korean chilies, sliced
1 tsp cumin seeds
1 tsp coriander seeds
1 tsp mixed peppercorns
1 cinnamon stick, bruised
3¾ cups vinegar
2 garlic cloves, crushed
2 tbsp dark brown sugar

Trim the eggplant and cut into small dice. Put into a bowl with the remaining vegetables, sprinkling each layer with salt. Cover and leave overnight.

Put the chilies, spices, vinegar, garlic and sugar into a pan and bring to a boil. Remove from the heat and pour into a clean bowl or jug. Cover and leave for at least 2 hours.

Rinse the vegetables well and drain thoroughly. Pack them into clean sterilized jars. Cover with the vinegar and seal. Keep for 2 weeks before using.

Thai Lettuce Packages ▶

Serves 4

8 oz Brie cheese
I large egg, beaten
2 cups fresh white bread crumbs
oil for deep-frying

Salsa
I tbsp sunflower oil
I small onion, finely chopped
I Hungarian cherry pepper, seeded
*   and finely chopped*
I red fresno chili, seeded and finely
*   chopped*
¾ cup finely chopped no-need-to-
*   soak dried apricots*
⅔ cup orange juice
fresh salad leaves, to garnish

Serves 4

I ripe melon, such as galia, seeded
arugula and radicchio leaves
8 oz shelled shrimp, thawed if frozen
2 red fresno chilies, seeded and sliced
few amatista (or fiesta) chilies,
*   to garnish*

Dressing
I tbsp soy sauce
2 tsp honey, warmed
salt and pepper
I tbsp tomato paste
I red fresno chili, roasted, seeded and
*   finely chopped*
2 tsp sesame oil
3 tbsp water

◀ *Deep-fried Brie with Spicy*
Apricot Salsa

DEEP-FRIED BRIE *with* SPICY APRICOT SALSA

Cut the Brie into 4 equal portions. Dip in the beaten egg, then coat in the bread crumbs. Cover lightly and place in the refrigerator while preparing the sauce.

Heat the sunflower oil in a pan and gently sauté the onion, cherry pepper and chili for 5 minutes. Add the apricots and orange juice, and simmer for 15 minutes, or until a chunky consistency is reached.

Heat the oil for deep-frying to 340°F and fry the Brie for 3 to 4 minutes, or until golden. Drain on paper towels. Serve with the apricot salsa, garnished with salad leaves.

SHRIMP *and* CHILI SALAD

Discard the skin of the melon and cut the flesh into thin wedges. Arrange the salad leaves on 4 individual plates and top with the melon slices and shrimp. Sprinkle with the sliced chilies.

Put all the ingredients for the dressing into a screw-top jar. Secure the lid and shake vigorously until well blended. Just before serving, drizzle the dressing over the melon and scatter the whole chilies on top.

HEAT 3-4

Serves 4

4 tbsp oil

2 garlic cloves, crushed

2 chawa chilies, seeded and sliced

I tsp ground coriander

I tsp ground cumin

½ tsp turmeric

I red onion, cut into thin wedges

I small red bell pepper, seeded and
   cut into thin strips

6 oz okra, trimmed and lightly pricked
   with a fork

1½ cups peeled, seeded and chopped
   tomatoes

1½ cups wiped and sliced oyster
   mushrooms

I tbsp freshly chopped cilantro

sour cream, to serve

WARM *and* SPICY SALAD

🌶 Heat the oil in a wok or large pan and stir-fry the garlic and chilies gently for 2 minutes. Add the spices and stir-fry for a further 1 minute.

🌶 Increase the heat slightly, then add the onion and pepper and cook for 2 minutes, stirring frequently. Add the okra, chopped tomatoes and mushrooms and stir-fry for a

further 3 minutes, or until the vegetables are cooked but still retain a bite.

🌶 Stir in the chopped cilantro and serve on individual plates, topped with spoonfuls of sour cream.

HEAT 5-6

Serves 4

I large cucumber, peeled

I small red onion, thinly sliced

2 or 3 red serrano chilies, seeded
   and thinly sliced

2 tbsp lime juice

I tbsp Thai fish sauce

2 tsp honey, warmed

I tbsp sesame oil

arugula leaves

⅓ cup shelled large roasted peanuts,
   roughly chopped

CUCUMBER SALAD *with* CHILIES

The dressing for this salad is traditionally made with dried shrimp. If using, grind 2 tablespoons of shrimp to a fine powder in a mortar and pestle, then add to the dressing and pour over the cucumbers.

🌶 Cut the cucumber in half lengthwise and cut into half-moon shapes. Place in a large shallow dish. Scatter the onion and chili slices over.

🌶 Mix together the lime juice, fish sauce, honey and oil. Pour over the cucumber and leave in a cool place for at least 30 minutes to allow the flavors to develop.

🌶 Arrange the arugula leaves on a serving platter, top with the cucumber mixture and sprinkle with the peanuts.

Cucumber Salad with Chilies ▶

HEAT 5

Serves 4

Dressing

6 dried chipotle chilies

1 small onion, sliced

2 garlic cloves, crushed

3 tbsp medium-dry white wine

3 tbsp white-wine vinegar

2 tbsp tomato paste

⅔ cup water

Salad

4 oz arugula

a few small frisée and radicchio leaves

1 heart of lettuce

2 heads red Belgian endive

4 oz baby spinach leaves

1 small red onion, thinly sliced

3 tbsp assorted fresh herbs, such as
    cilantro, flat-leafed parsley,
    oregano and marjoram

MIXED SALAD LEAVES *with* CHIPOTLE CHILI DRESSING

Chipotle chilies give a delicious smoky flavor to the dressing. You can substitute any other dried chili, if preferred, or use fresno chilies for a fresher flavor.

➤ Split the chilies and discard the seeds. Put into a pan with the remaining dressing ingredients over gentle heat and cook, covered, for 45 minutes, or until the chilies are soft and liquid is reduced by half.

➤ Blend to a smooth purée in a blender or food processor and then pass through a strainer to remove any seeds. Reserve.

➤ Lightly rinse all the salad leaves, the endive and herbs and pat dry with paper towels. Tear the leaves if large, then toss together in a salad bowl.

➤ Divide the endive into single leaves and add to the salad with the onion and herbs. Mix together lightly. Just before serving, drizzle with the dressing and toss lightly.

ONION *and* CHILI BAHJIS

HEAT 6–7

Serves 4

2 cups chick-pea or all-purpose flour

I tsp turmeric

2 tsp ground cumin

2 tsp ground coriander

I tsp salt

4 green jalapeño chilies, seeded and
finely chopped

2 garlic cloves, crushed

2 onions, coarsely grated

6 scallions, trimmed and finely
chopped

about ⅔ cup iced water

vegetable oil for deep-frying

sprigs of fresh cilantro, to garnish

🌶 Sift the flour, spices and salt into a bowl, then stir in the chopped chilies, garlic, onions and scallions.

🌶 Mix to a soft dropping consistency with the iced water.

🌶 Heat the oil to 325°F and carefully drop in small spoonfuls of the batter. Cook for 2 minutes, or until golden. Drain on paper towels and serve garnished with sprigs of cilantro.

PICKLED BOK CHOY

HEAT 6

Makes 4 x I-lb jars

2 heads bok choy

I tbsp salt

2½ cups white wine or rice vinegar

2 tbsp finely chopped peeled
gingerroot

3 garlic cloves, crushed

1½ cups light soft brown sugar

3 or 4 Korean chilies, seeded and
sliced

This is similar to the Korean Kimchi pickle which is designed to "pep up" the appetite. It is traditionally served every day in Korea and northern China.

🌶 Rinse the bok choy and cut off the stems. (Use the remaining leaves in salads and stir-fries.) Cut the stems into strips about 2 inches long. Place in a colander, sprinkling each layer with salt. Leave to stand for 30 minutes. Rinse thoroughly and drain well. Pack into clean, sterilized jars.

🌶 Put the vinegar, ginger, garlic, sugar and chilies into a pan and heat until the sugar has dissolved. Bring to a boil, then pour over the bok choy. Allow to cool, then cover.

🌶 Let the pickle stand at room temperature for 2 to 4 days before using, pushing the leaves down under the liquid once a day. Allow the air bubbles to escape. Keeps in the refrigerator for up to 1 month. Drain before serving.

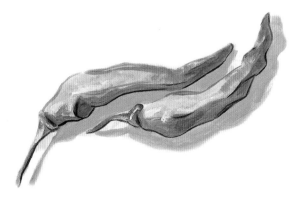

RANCH-STYLE EGGS

Huevos rancheros

Serves 4

4 tbsp corn oil

4 wheat or corn flour tortillas

3 shallots, finely chopped

1 garlic clove, crushed

1 or 2 red New Mexico chilies,
   seeded and chopped

1½ cups peeled, seeded and chopped
   ripe tomatoes

1 tbsp tomato paste

2 tbsp water

salt and pepper

4 eggs

4 tbsp refried beans

sprigs of parsley, to garnish

Traditionally, this was served as a breakfast dish in Mexico, but it is now served at any time, often with refried beans.

➣ Heat 1 tsp of the oil in a skillet and fry a tortilla for 30 seconds on both sides until crisp. Drain and keep warm. Repeat until all the tortillas have been fried.

➣ Heat 2 tbsp of the remaining oil and sauté the shallots, garlic and chilies for 5 minutes. Add the tomatoes and tomato paste blended with the water and leave to simmer while cooking the eggs.

➣ Heat the remaining oil and fry the eggs until cooked as preferred. Place a tortilla on a plate, top with an egg and some tomato sauce. Serve with refried beans and garnish with parsley.

SAUTÉED MUSHROOMS *with* CHILI SALSA

HEAT 4

Serves 4

6 tbsp virgin olive oil

I garlic clove, crushed

2 de agua chilies, seeded and sliced

2 shallots, thinly sliced

2½ cups wiped and sliced assorted
    wild mushrooms

4 oz button mushrooms, wiped

1½ cups peeled, seeded and chopped
    plum tomatoes

I tbsp freshly chopped basil

salt and pepper

I ciabatta loaf, sliced

Salsa Rojo (page 46)

sprigs of fresh basil, to garnish

❧ Heat 4 tbsp of the oil in a skillet and gently sauté the garlic, chilies and shallots for 5 minutes, or until the shallots are soft and transparent.

❧ Add the mushrooms and continue to cook for 4 to 5 minutes. Stir in the tomatoes, basil and seasoning to taste and heat through for 1 to 2 minutes.

❧ Meanwhile, drizzle the ciabatta slices with the remaining oil and broil lightly. Arrange the mushroom mixture on the toasted bread and serve with Salsa Rojo. Garnish with sprigs of basil.

VEGETABLE SAMOSAS

HEAT 4–5

Serves 4

¾ cup finely diced potatoes

I tbsp corn or sunflower oil

I onion, finely chopped

I garlic clove, crushed

2 red Anaheim chilies, seeded and
    finely chopped

I bird's eye (Thai) chili, seeded and
    very finely chopped

I tsp ground cumin

I tsp ground coriander

I cup shelled peas, thawed if frozen

I red bell pepper, seeded and diced

I tbsp apricot or fruit chutney

I tbsp freshly chopped cilantro

4 sheets filo pastry dough

vegetable oil for deep-frying

chili flowers (page 11) and fresh
    cilantro, to garnish

❧ Cook the diced potatoes in boiling salted water for 5 to 8 minutes, or until just cooked, Drain and reserve.

❧ Heat the corn or sunflower oil in a skillet and gently sauté the onion, garlic and chilies for 3 minutes. Add the spices and sauté for a further 3 minutes.

❧ Remove from the heat and stir in the potatoes, peas, red bell pepper, chutney and chopped cilantro. Mix together well.

❧ Cut the filo pastry sheets in half lengthwise to make 8 strips, each 10 x 4 inches. Place 1½ tbsp of the filling at one end of each strip and fold over diagonally to form a triangle. Continue folding along the strip, sealing the edges with water.

❧ Heat the oil to 325°F and fry the samosas in batches for about 5 minutes, or until golden. Drain on paper towels. Serve hot or cold, garnished with chili flowers and sprigs of cilantro.

Sautéed Mushrooms with Chili Salsa ▶

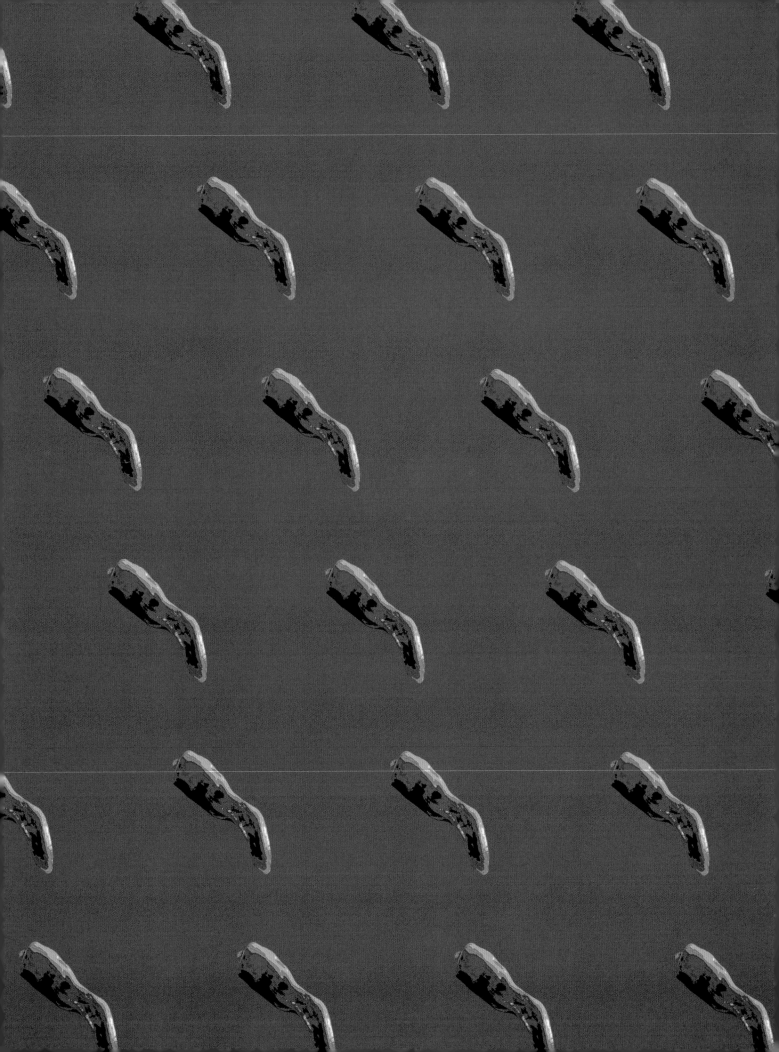

Chapter 3

Sauces and
Relishes

CHILI MAYONNAISE

HEAT 4–5

Makes about ¾ cup

2 large egg yolks

½ to 1 tsp salt

½ to 1 tsp mustard powder

½ to 1 tsp Red Chili Paste (page 47)

¼ tsp freshly ground pepper

⅔ cup olive oil

1 to 2 tbsp strained lime juice

🌶 Put the egg yolks, salt, pepper, mustard powder and Red Chili Paste into a food processor and switch on to a low speed. Add the olive oil, drop by drop to begin with, then as the mayonnaise thickens, increase to a very thin steady stream. If the mayonnaise is becoming too thick, add a little lime juice.

🌶 When all the oil has been added, stir in the lime juice. Cover and chill until required. Use within 1 week of making.

CHILI SEASONING

HEAT 5

Makes 4 to 5 tbsps

2 dried ancho chilies

6 dried ají mirasol chilies

1 tsp paprika pepper

3 tbsp coarse sea salt

finely grated peel of 1 lemon

🌶 Discard the stems and seeds from the chilies, then place in a nonstick skillet and fry gently for 3 minutes, shaking the pan occasionally to ensure they do not burn.

🌶 Remove from the heat, put the chilies into a bowl and cover with almost boiling water. Cover and leave for 15 to 20 minutes. Drain and pat dry with paper towels until thoroughly dry.

🌶 Place in a mortar and pestle or a coffee grinder and pound or grind to a paste. Add the paprika, salt and lemon peel and continue to process until a fine consistency is reached.

🌶 Pack into small containers, cover and use as required. Store in a cool, dark place.

CHILI BUTTER

HEAT 2–3

Makes ½ cup

½ cup unsalted butter, softened

1 green fresno chili, seeded and finely chopped

1 to 2 tsp lime juice

1 to 2 tsp Chili Seasoning (see above)

1 tbsp freshly chopped cilantro

Ideal for use with corn-on-the cob, fish, steaks, chicken and pork dishes.

🌶 Put all the ingredients into a bowl and beat until thoroughly blended.

🌶 Shape into a 1-inch roll and wrap in waxed paper. Chill until required.

SPICY GROUND BEEF SAUCE

Picadillo

Serves 4

1 tbsp corn or olive oil

1 onion, finely chopped

2 garlic cloves, crushed

2 Scotch bonnet chilies, seeded and chopped

2 celery stalks, trimmed and finely chopped

12 oz minced beef

1 tbsp tomato paste

2 tbsp water

1½ cups peeled and chopped ripe tomatoes

1 tsp ground coriander

1 tsp ground cumin

2 tbsp cider vinegar

1 tsp honey

2 tbsp freshly chopped oregano

Kenyan chilies could be used in this dish if available, for a milder sauce. Use in tacos, enchiladas or burritos, over pasta or with rice.

Heat the oil in a skillet and sauté the onion, garlic, chilies and celery for 5 minutes. Add the beef and cook, stirring frequently, for 5 to 8 minutes, or until browned.

Blend the tomato paste with the water and add to the pan with the remaining ingredients. Bring to a boil, then reduce the heat and simmer for 45 minutes, or until a thick consistency is reached.

RED CHILI SAUCE

Salsa rojo

Makes about 1½ cups

3 red serrano chilies

1 tbsp corn or olive oil

4 ripe tomatoes, peeled, seeded and
 chopped

4 shallots, finely chopped

2 garlic cloves, chopped

1 tsp ground cumin

1 tsp ground coriander

⅔ cup vegetable or chicken stock

2 tbsp tomato paste

½ tsp salt

½ tsp freshly ground pepper

1 tbsp lime juice

2 tbsp freshly chopped cilantro

Both Green and Red Chili Sauce are used as a condiment to fish, meat and poultry or can be used as a dip.

Preheat the broiler. Place the chilies in the broiler pan and drizzle with the oil. Broil for 5 minutes, or until blackened and blistered. Put into a plastic bag and leave to sweat for 10 minutes, then discard the skins and chop.

Put all the ingredients, except the cilantro, into a food processor and blend to a thick consistency.

Pour into a skillet and cook over gentle heat, stirring frequently, for 10 minutes. (Add a little extra stock or water if consistency is too thick.)

(Clockwise from top left) ▶
Red Chili Paste, Chili Pepper Relish,
Green Chili Sauce, Red Chili Sauce

Makes about 2 cups

1 lb green Anaheim chilies
1 large onion, quartered
3 garlic cloves, peeled
2 tbsp corn or olive oil
1¼ cups chicken or vegetable stock
1 tsp salt
½ tsp black pepper
2 tbsp freshly chopped cilantro
thinly sliced chili, to garnish

Makes about 1¼ cups

1½ cups peeled, seeded and chopped
   ripe tomatoes
2 shallots, finely chopped
2 or 3 red serrano chilies, seeded and
   chopped
1 garlic clove, crushed
1 tsp salt
3 tbsp freshly chopped cilantro
1 tbsp lime juice or cider vinegar
3-inch piece cucumber, peeled and
   finely chopped
1 tbsp pumpkin seeds, roasted and
   then finely ground
cilantro sprigs, to garnish

Makes 5 tbsp

4 red habanero chilies, seeded
1 onion, chopped
2 garlic cloves, crushed
2 tsp ground coriander
1 tbsp freshly chopped cilantro
1-inch piece gingerroot, peeled and
   grated
grated peel and juice of 2 limes
1 tsp salt
½ tsp black pepper
3 tbsp corn or olive oil

GREEN CHILI SAUCE

Salsa verde

Ideal to serve with egg dishes, chicken or as the basis of a stew or casserole.

Preheat the broiler. Place the chilies, onion and garlic in the broiler pan and drizzle with the oil. Grill for 5 to 8 minutes, or until the chilies have blistered and the skins blackened. Put the chilies into a plastic bag and leave to sweat for about 10 minutes, then discard the skins.

Put the chilies and all the other ingredients, except the cilantro, into a food processor and blend to form a chunky purée. Stir in the cilantro and warm through just before serving. Garnish with sliced chili.

CHILI PEPPER RELISH

If liked, this can be served as an appetizer with crudités and taco chips.

Put the tomatoes into a bowl and stir in the shallots, chilies, garlic, salt, cilantro and lime juice or vinegar. Mix together well, then cover and leave for at least 30 minutes to allow the flavors to develop.

Stir in the cucumber and pumpkin seeds. Garnish with the cilantro sprigs.

RED CHILI PASTE

Use when extra heat is required in order to spice up soups, stews and casseroles. Add toward the end of cooking time to give a distinctive and fiery flavor. Not suitable for freezing.

Rinse the chilies and put into the top of a steamer over a pan of gently steaming water.

Steam for 5 minutes or until soft. Alternatively, cover with boiling water and leave for 15 minutes, then drain.

Put all the ingredients into a food processor and blend to form a thick paste, adding a little extra oil if necessary. Transfer to a screw-top jar and store in the refrigerator. Use within 1 week.

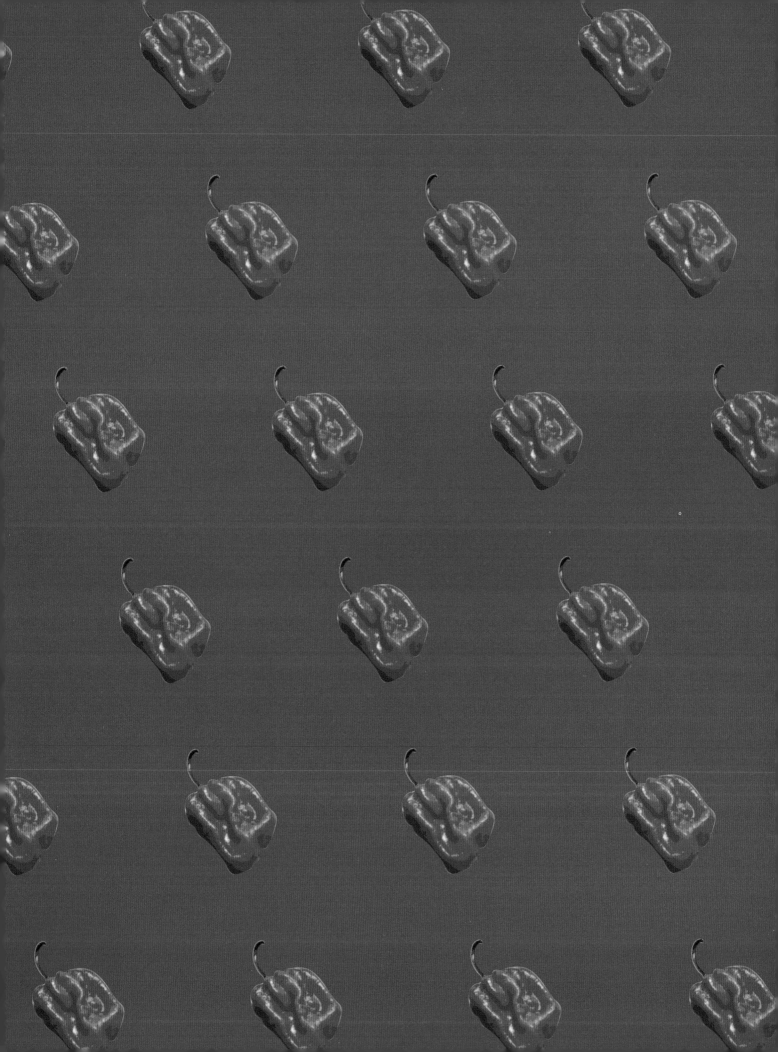

Potatoes
and Rice

Serves 4

4½ cups potatoes, cut into chunks

salt and pepper

2 tbsp milk

2 tbsp butter

4 red Anaheim chilies, peeled, seeded
    and finely chopped

6 scallions, trimmed and finely
    chopped

extra chopped scallions, to garnish

Serves 4

1 large or 2 medium fresh pineapple

2 tbsp sunflower oil

1 red bell pepper, seeded and
    chopped

1½ cups zucchini, trimmed and diced

6 scallions, trimmed and sliced
    diagonally

2 cups cooked long-grain rice

6 canned jalapeño chilies, drained and
    chopped

salt and pepper

2 tbsp pine nuts, toasted

3 tbsp freshly chopped cilantro

grated cheese, to serve

Serves 4

2 tbsp sunflower oil

3 red New Mexico chilies, roasted,
    seeded and chopped

1½ cups cooked long-grain rice

¾ cup shelled peas, blanched

salt

4 oz shelled shrimp, thawed if frozen

2 large eggs, beaten

2 scallions, trimmed and chopped

SAVORY MASHED POTATOES

Cook the potatoes in boiling salted water for 15 minutes, or until tender. Drain, then add the seasoning and milk, and mash until smooth.

Melt the butter in a large pan and gently sauté the chilies and scallions for 3 minutes.

Add the mashed potatoes and stir well. Heat through for 5 to 6 minutes, stirring occasionally, until piping hot. Place in a serving dish and fork the top. Sprinkle with a little extra chopped scallions. Serve immediately.

PINEAPPLE *and* CHILI RICE

Cut the pineapple in half lengthwise through the plume and scoop out the flesh. Reserve the two halves. Discard the central core, dice the remaining flesh and reserve.

Heat the oil in a pan and sauté the red pepper and zucchini for 5 minutes, or until softened. Add the scallions and sauté for a further 1 minute. Stir in the rice with the canned chilies, seasoning and the reserved pineapple flesh.

Heat gently, stirring occasionally, for 5 minutes, or until hot. Then stir in the pine nuts and cilantro. Pile into the reserved pineapple shells and serve with grated cheese.

FRIED CHILI RICE

The staple food ingredient for the Chinese is rice, which forms the basis of much of their traditional cuisine. If preferred, use Thai or Korean chilies, but as they are fiercer in heat, either reduce the quantity or be prepared for a taste explosion.

Heat the oil in a large skillet and gently sauté the chilies for 1 minute. Add the cooked rice and heat through, stirring frequently, for 3 minutes.

Stir in the peas, salt and shrimp, then pour the eggs over and increase the heat. Cook, stirring constantly, for 2 to 3 minutes, or until the eggs have set. Serve immediately, sprinkled with the chopped scallions.

Pineapple and Chili Rice ▶

HEAT 5

Serves 4

2 tbsp sunflower oil

1 red onion, chopped

2 garlic cloves, chopped

5 red Anaheim chilies, seeded nd
  chopped

6 sun-dried tomatoes, chopped

¾ to 3¾ cups vegetable stock

1 cup long-grain rice

1 red bell pepper, seeded and
  chopped

2 tbsp tomato paste

salt and pepper

¾ cup whole kernel corn

freshly chopped cilantro, to garnish

HEAT 5

Serves 4

2 tbsp sunflower oil

1 large onion, chopped

2 garlic cloves, chopped

4 green Anaheim chilies, seeded and
  sliced

1 cup long-grain white rice

1 green bell pepper, seeded and
  chopped

2½ cups vegetable stock

salt and pepper

¾ cup frozen peas

1 tbsp freshly chopped parsley

2 tbsp pumpkin seeds, toasted

RED RICE

Arroz rojo

✎ Preheat the oven to 350°F.

✎ Heat the oil in a pan and gently sauté the onion, garlic, chilies and sun-dried tomatoes for 3 minutes. Add 1¼ cups of the stock and simmer for 10 minutes, or until the tomatoes are soft. Blend in a food processor, then transfer to a skillet.

✎ Add the rice, red pepper and the tomato paste blended with 2 tbsp of the stock. Put into a flameproof casserole with 2 cups of the stock and seasoning to taste.

✎ Bring to a boil, then cover and place in the oven. Cook for 30 minutes. Add the corn kernels with extra stock if necessary and cook for a further 10 minutes, or until the rice is cooked. Separate the grains with a fork and serve sprinkled with the cilantro.

GREEN RICE

Arroz verde

Rice forms a staple part of many different cuisines, offering a nutritious, yet relatively cheap, food. In all countries where rice grows abundantly, many different recipes have been evolved, all using other ingredients that are plentiful to the relevant country.

✎ Heat the oil in a large skillet and sauté the onion, garlic and chilies for 3 minutes. Add the rice and green bell pepper, and sauté for a further 3 minutes.

✎ Pour in the stock and bring to a boil. Reduce the heat and simmer for 15 minutes, or until the rice is almost tender. Add a little more stock if necesary and stir occasionally during cooking.

✎ Stir in the peas and seasoning to taste, and cook for a further 5 to 7 minutes, or until the rice and peas are cooked. Adjust the seasoning and serve sprinkled with the parsley and toasted pumpkin seeds.

◄ Red Rice
  Green Rice

Serves 6

2 tbsp sunflower oil

2 garlic cloves, crushed

4 red de agua chilies, seeded and
    chopped

heaped ¾ cup short-grain rice

1 large carrot, grated

2 tbsp tomato paste

2 tbsp water

2½ cups vegetable stock

salt and pepper

7-oz can red kidney beans, drained
    and rinsed

½ cup whole-corn kernel

2 tbsp freshly chopped cilantro

2 tsp olive oil

1 large tomato, sliced

6 buns, lightly toasted

Chili Pepper Relish (page 47), to serve

CHILI-RICE BURGERS

Heat the sunflower oil in a skillet and sauté the garlic and chilies for 5 minutes. Add the rice and continue to cook for 3 minutes, stirring occasionally. Stir in the carrot.

Blend the tomato paste with the water and stir into the pan with the stock. Add seasoning and bring to a boil. Reduce the heat and simmer for 20 minutes, or until the rice is cooked, stirring occasionally and adding a little extra stock if the rice is very dry.

Add the kidney beans and corn kernels, and cook for a further 5 minutes. (The mixture needs to be very stiff so that it will stick together.) Stir in the chopped cilantro and remove from the heat. Allow to cool.

When the mixture is cool enough to handle, wet your hands slightly and shape into 6 large burgers. Cover and chill for at least 30 minutes.

Preheat the broiler to medium. Place the burgers under the broiler and brush lightly with a little olive oil. Broil for 4 to 5 minutes, or until heated through, carefully turning the burgers over once during cooking.

Place a slice of tomato on the bottom of each bun and top with a rice burger. Spoon a little relish over, cover with the bun tops and serve with extra Chili Pepper Relish.

Serves 4

1 tsp cumin seeds

1 tsp whole coriander seeds

1 tsp fenugreek seeds

5 cloves

6 cardamom pods

2 tbsp sunflower oil

1 large onion, sliced

2 garlic cloves, crushed

4 red jalapeño chilies, seeded and
    chopped

4½ cups cubed potatoes

2½ cups vegetable stock

1 red bell pepper, skinned, seeded and
    sliced

2 tbsp freshly chopped cilantro

POTATO CURRY

Put the whole spices in a mortar or food processor and grind to a powder.

Heat the oil in a large pan and sauté the onion, garlic and chilies for 5 minutes, or until softened. Add the ground spices and cook gently for a further 3 minutes, stirring occasionally.

Add the potatoes with the stock and bring to a boil. Cover the pan, reduce the heat and simmer for 15 minutes, or until the potatoes are tender.

Add the sliced red bell pepper and cook for a further 5 minutes. Stir in the freshly chopped cilantro and serve immediately.

POTATOES *with* CHILI, PEANUTS AND CHEESE

HEAT 5

Serves 4

4½ cups finely diced potatoes

1 large onion, sliced

2 garlic cloves, chopped

5 red fresno chilies

4 to 5 tbsp olive oil

salt and pepper

1 cup shelled raw peanuts

shavings of grated Parmesan cheese

Preheat the oven to 400°C.

Put the potatoes in a roasting pan and scatter the onion and garlic over.

Make a slit down each chili and discard the seeds. Chop roughly. Add to the vegetables and sprinkle with the oil, then add the seasoning. Turn the vegetables in the oil and roast in the oven for 50 minutes, turning the vegetables occasionally.

Scatter the peanuts over and continue to roast until cooked and golden. Serve sprinkled with Parmesan cheese.

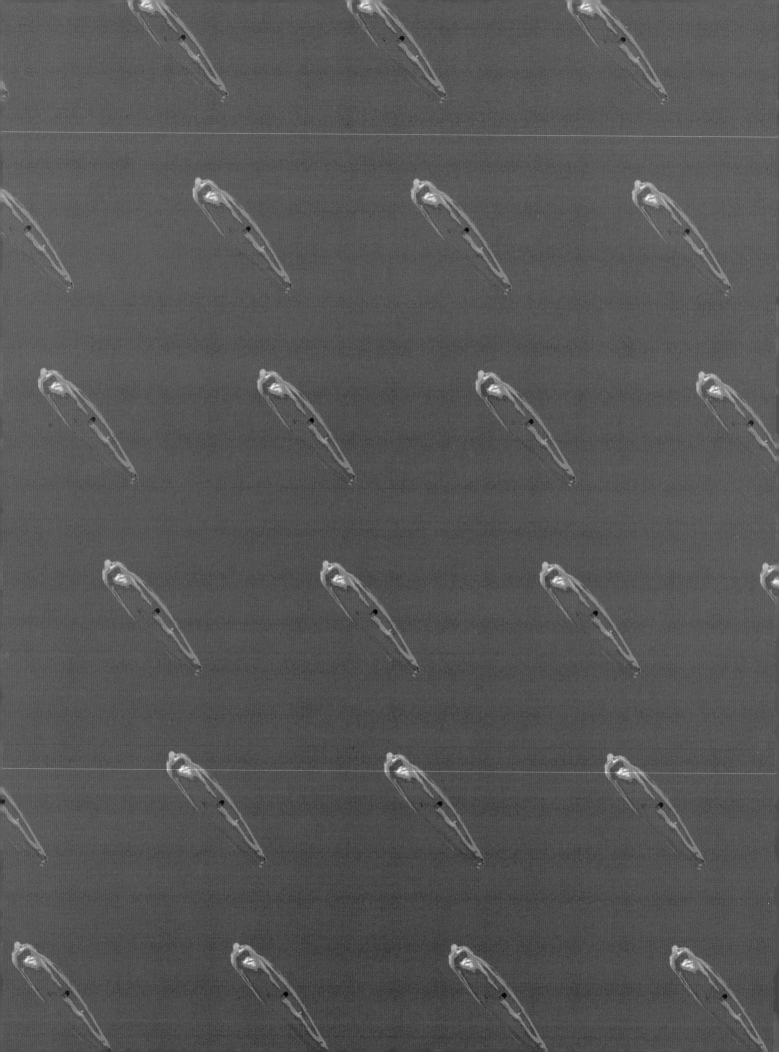

Fish

HEAT 5

Serves 4

4 salmon steaks, about 6 oz each
1 small onion, sliced
2 bay leaves
few sprigs of parsley
4 or 5 black peppercorns
⅔ cup dry white wine
1 tbsp white-wine vinegar
⅔ cup water

Sauce

2 tbsp olive oil
1 garlic clove, crushed
1-inch piece gingerroot, peeled and
    grated
1 cup shelled raw peanuts
2 red Thai chilies, seeded and sliced
2 tsp dark brown sugar
1¼ cups vegetable stock
1 tbsp lemon juice
lemon twists, to garnish

SALMON STEAKS *with* THAI-STYLE SAUCE

Wipe the salmon and reserve. Place the onion, bay leaves, parsley, peppercorns, wine and vinegar in a skillet. Add the water and bring to a boil. Reduce the heat and simmer for 10 minutes. Strain and reserve the liquid until ready to cook the fish.

Heat the oil for the sauce in the skillet and sauté the garlic and ginger for 2 minutes. Add the peanuts and fry gently for 10 minutes, or until golden.

Put the peanuts and chilies with garlic, ginger and oil in a food processor with the remaining sauce ingredients. Blend to a purée,

then return to the cleaned pan and simmer for 8 to 10 minutes, or until reduced slightly. Keep warm while cooking the fish.

When ready to cook the fish, reheat the reserved liquid in the skillet and add the fish. Bring to a boil, then cover and reduce the heat to a very gentle simmer. Cook for 3 to 4 minutes, or until the fish is cooked. Drain and arrange on serving plates and spoon a little of the sauce over. Garnish with lemon twists.

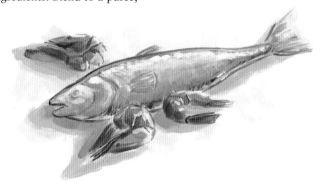

HEAT 4–5

Serves 4

2 garlic cloves, crushed
4 shallots, finely chopped
1-inch piece gingerroot, peeled and
    grated
3 red fresno chilies, seeded and finely
    chopped
6 ají mirasol dried chilies, roasted and
    rehydrated (page 16)
2 tbsp corn or sunflower oil
1 lb white crabmeat, drained if canned
⅔ cup coconut milk
1 tbsp cornstarch
2 tbsp water
⅔ cup crème fraîche
chili flowers (page 11) and lemon
    wedges, to garnish

CRAB *in* RICH COCONUT MILK SAUCE

Put the garlic, shallots, ginger, fresh and rehydrated dried chilies into a food processor and blend to a paste. Alternatively, use a mortar and pestle.

Heat the oil in a wok or large pan and gently fry the paste for 3 minutes, taking care not to burn it. Add the crabmeat and heat through for 3 minutes, stirring frequently.

Pour in the coconut milk and bring to a boil. Blend the cornstarch to a smooth paste with the water and stir into the crabmeat mixture. Cook, stirring constantly, until the sauce thickens. Add the crème fraîche and heat through for 1 to 2 minutes. Garnish with chili flowers and lemon wedges, and serve with plenty of warm crusty bread.

Salmon Steaks with ▶
Thai-style Sauce

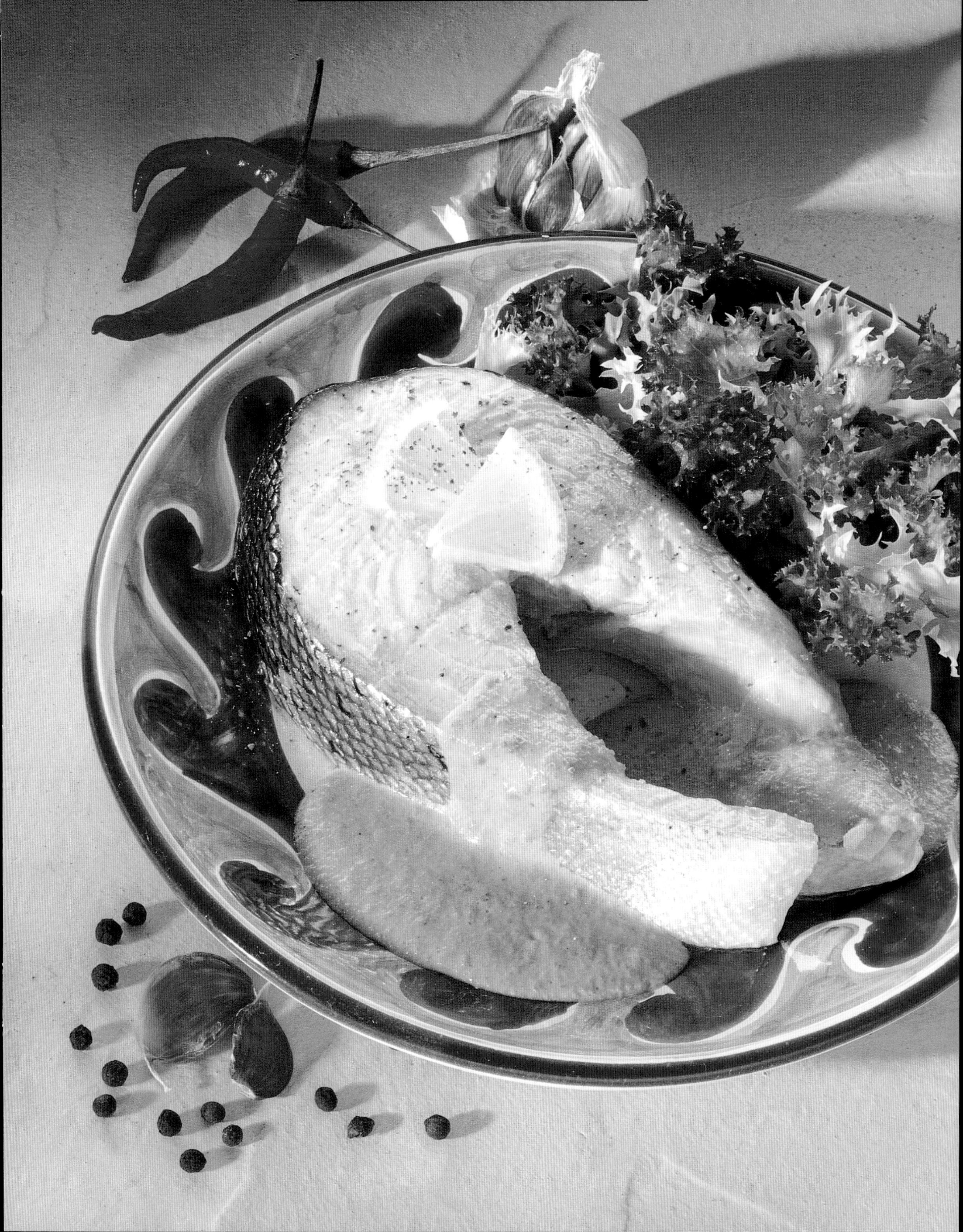

SEAFOOD GUMBO

HEAT 7-8

Serves 4

2 tbsp corn or sunflower oil

I large onion, chopped

2 garlic cloves, crushed

2–3 Jamaican hot chilies, seeded and chopped

2 celery stalks, trimmed and chopped

2 red bell peppers, seeded and sliced

4 oz slab bacon, chopped

2 tbsp filé powder or flour

3 smoked pork sausages or Italian sausages, cut into chunks

1½ cups peeled and chopped tomatoes

1½ cups trimmed and sliced okra

2½ cups chicken stock

8 oz monkfish, central bone and skin removed and cubed

8 oz raw shrimp, shelled and deveined

8 oz squid, prepared (page 66) and sliced

½ to1 tsp hot-pepper sauce

salt and pepper

heaped I cup freshly cooked long-grain rice

2 tbsp freshly chopped parsley, to garnish the rice

Gumbos vary from region to region; there are no hard and fast rules. One of the staple ingredients is okra, or lady's fingers. The filé powder is used as a thickening agent; plain flour can be used instead.

Heat the oil in a large pan and gently sauté the onion, garlic, chilies and celery for 5 minutes, or until soft.

Add the sliced red bell peppers and the bacon, and sauté for a further 3 minutes. Sprinkle in the filé powder or flour and cook gently for a further 3 minutes.

Add the sausages, tomatoes, okra and stock, then bring to a boil. Reduce the heat and simmer for 10 minutes, stirring occasionally. Add the monkfish and simmer for a further 10 minutes, or until the fish is almost tender.

Stir in the shrimp, squid, hot-pepper sauce and seasoning to taste, and cook for 5 to 7 minutes, or until all the fish is cooked through and flakes easily.

(Take care not to overcook the squid.)

Finally add the rice and parsley. Heat through for 5 to 7 minutes and serve.

ROAST MONKFISH

HEAT 5-6

Serves 4

1½ lb piece monkfish, skinned

4 red fresno chilies, seeded and cut into strips

I red onion, sliced

3 large carrots, sliced

6 celery stalks, trimmed and chopped

2 or 3 fresh bay leaves

salt and pepper

2 tbsp sunflower or olive oil

⅔ cup fish or vegetable stock

freshly chopped parsley and thinly sliced, seeded red fresno chili, to garnish

Preheat the oven to 350°F.

Using a sharp knife, cut the monkfish away from the bone that runs down its center and discard the bone. Rinse and pat dry with paper towels. Then make small slits down the monkfish fillets on all sides and insert the strips of chili.

Place the vegetables with the bay leaves on a large sheet of foil and place the fish on top.

Season with salt and pepper. Pour the oil and stock over, and fold the foil over, completely encasing the fish. Place in a roasting pan.

Bake for 20 to 25 minutes, or until the fish is cooked through and flakes easily. Baste occasionally during roasting. Discard the bay leaves and serve garnished with the cooked vegetables.

◄ Seafood Gumbo

HEAT 3-4

Serves 6

8 oz prepared piecrust dough

I tbsp corn or sunflower oil

I onion, finely chopped

2 to 3 red Anaheim chilies, seeded and
  sliced

4 oz slab bacon, rinded and cut into
  strips

8 oz white crabmeat, flaked

4 oz shelled shrimp, thawed if frozen

2 large eggs

⅔ cup light cream

salt and pepper

HEAT 5-6

Serves 4

8 to 12 canned large green chilies,
  drained

8 oz shelled shrimp, thawed if frozen
  and finely chopped

4 scallions, trimmed and chopped

3 green jalapeño chilies, seeded and
  finely chopped

½ cup grated hard cheese, such as
  Cheddar

I small red apple, cored and finely
  chopped

grated peel of I lemon

salt and pepper

3 to 4 tbsp prepared mayonnaise

salad leaves and sliced red jalapeño
  chilies, to garnish

SHELLFISH-CHILI QUICHE

▄ Preheat the oven to 400°F.

▄ Roll out the dough on a lightly floured surface and use to line an 8-inch loose-bottomed tart pan. Place a sheet of waxed paper and baking beans in the bottom and bake blind for 12 minutes. Remove the paper and beans and continue baking for a further 5 minutes. Reduce the oven temperature to 350°F.

▄ Meanwhile, heat the oil in a skillet and sauté the onion and chilies for 2 minutes. Add the bacon and sauté for a further 3 minutes. Drain, then arrange the bacon mixture on the bottom of the quiche shell.

▄ Place the crabmeat on top of the bacon mixture with the shrimp. Beat the eggs with the cream and seasoning to taste, then pour over the crabmeat. Bake for 20 to 25 minutes, or until set.

SHRIMP RELLENOS

"Rellenos" is a Spanish word meaning stuffed. If canned chilies are unavailable, use large fresh ones that have been seeded and blanched.

▄ Pat the canned chilies dry with paper towels and make a slit down one side. Discard the seeds if necessary, then rinse and pat dry again.

▄ Mix the shrimp, scallions, chilies, cheese, apple and lemon peel together with seasoning to taste. Add the mayonnaise and mix together well.

▄ Use the shrimp mixture to stuff the chilies. Arrange on a serving platter and garnish with salad leaves and chilies.

Shrimp Rellenos ▶

HEAT 4–5

Serves 4

24 live clams, scrubbed and any open
    ones discarded

1 tbsp sunflower oil

1 red onion, thinly sliced

4 de agua red chilies, seeded and
    sliced

finely shredded peel of 1 lime

1-inch piece gingerroot, peeled and
    grated

2 garlic cloves, crushed

1 tbsp Thai fish sauce

4 tbsp coconut milk

1¼ cups fish or vegetable stock

1 tbsp cornstarch

3 tbsp cold water

1 tbsp freshly chopped mint

1 tbsp freshly chopped basil

CLAMS *with* CHILI *and* HERBS

Put the clams into a large bowl, cover with cold water and set aside in a cool place.

Heat the oil in a wok or large pan and sauté the onion, chilies, lime peel, ginger and garlic for 2 minutes. Add the fish sauce, coconut milk and stock. Drain the clams and add to the pan. Bring to a boil, then cover the pan and reduce the heat. Simmer for 3 to 5 minutes, shaking the pan or stirring occasionally.

Blend the cornstarch with the water and add to the pan with the herbs. Cook, stirring, until the stock thickens. Discard any clams that have not opened and serve.

HEAT 5

Serves 4

¾ cup pumpkin seeds

1 small onion, chopped

6 tomatoes, peeled, seeded and
    chopped

2 green jalapeño chilies

2 tbsp honey

1¼ cups fish or vegetable stock

1 tbsp freshly chopped cilantro

salt and black pepper

2 tbsp tomato paste, blended with
    4 tbsp water

1 lb raw jumbo shrimp, thawed if
    frozen, shelled, tails left
    intact and deveined

fresh cilantro sprigs, to garnish

freshly cooked rice or warm bread, to
    serve

HEAT 6–7

Serves 4

2 tbsp oil

1 large onion, chopped

2 garlic cloves, crushed

4 to 5 rocotillo chili peppers, seeded

2 celery stalks, trimmed and chopped

1 red bell pepper, seeded and sliced

1 green bell pepper, seeded and sliced

2 tbsp tomato paste

2 tbsp water

1¼ cups fish or chicken stock

14 oz-can crushed tomatoes

1 tsp Worcestershire sauce

salt and pepper

8 oz white fish fillets, such as cod

8 oz mackerel fillets

1 tbsp freshly chopped oregano

1 tbsp freshly chopped marjoram

juice of ½ lime

4 oz shelled raw shrimp

sprigs of fresh oregano or marjoram,
    to garnish

freshly cooked rice and green salad, to
    serve

SHRIMP *with* PUMPKIN SEEDS

Camarones en pepitas

Pumpkin seeds are widely used in Mexican cooking, nearly always toasted and then ground to a powder.

➥ Preheat the broiler to medium and spread the pumpkin seeds over the broiler pan. Toast for 2 to 3 minutes, stirring frequently to prevent them burning. Remove from the broiler and allow to cool.

➥ Put the toasted seeds into a food processor and grind finely. Alternatively, pound in a mortar and pestle. Put the remaining ingredients, except the tomato paste and shrimp, into the food processor and blend together.

➥ Put the blended ingredients with the tomato paste into a pan and bring to a gentle boil. Reduce the heat and add the shrimp. Heat through gently for 3 to 5 minutes, or until the shrimp are cooked. Do not allow the mixture to boil, otherwise the shrimp will become tough. Garnish with sprigs of cilantro and serve immediately with freshly cooked rice or warm bread.

MIXED FISH, CREOLE STYLE

➥ Heat the oil in a large pan and sauté the onion, garlic, chilies and celery for 5 minutes, or until softened. Add the peppers and cook for a further 3 minutes.

➥ Blend the tomato paste with the water and stir into the pan with the stock, chopped tomatoes, Worcestershire sauce and seasoning to taste. Bring to a boil, then reduce the heat and simmer for about 20 minutes, or until the sauce has reduced and is thick.

➥ Skin the fish fillets and discard any bones. Cut the fish into bite-sized pieces. Rinse and pat dry with paper towels.

➥ Add the fish with the herbs and lime juice to the pan and simmer for a further 6 minutes. Add the shrimp and cook for a further 4 minutes, or until the fish is tender and flaked through. Garnish with the herbs and serve with freshly cooked rice and a tossed green salad.

HEAT 6-7

Serves 4

1½ lb white firm fish fillets, such as
  monkfish or cod
2 tbsp corn oil
1 large onion, chopped
3 garlic cloves, crushed
4 rocotillo chilies, seeded and sliced
4 dried pasilla chilies, roasted,
  rehydrated and ground to a paste
1 tsp ground cumin
1 tsp ground coriander
1 tsp turmeric
14-oz can crushed tomatoes
2 tbsp tomato paste
4 tbsp water
3 tbsp lemon juice
2 tbsp freshly chopped cilantro
freshly cooked rice and
  accompaniments, to serve

HEAT 8–10

Serves 4

1½ lb squid
2 shallots, chopped
2 garlic cloves, crushed
2 red habanero chilies, seeded and
  chopped
4 dried ancho chilies, roasted and
  rehydrated (page 16)
2 tbsp corn or sunflower oil
2¼ cups peeled, seeded and chopped
  plum tomatoes
juice of 2 limes
2 to 3 tsp soft brown sugar
a few sprigs of fresh oregano

CURRIED COD *with* CHILI PEPPERS

If liked, the dried chilies can be replaced with 3 or 4 fresno chilies.

Remove any bones from the fish. Rinse, pat dry with paper towels and cut into cubes.

Heat the oil in a large pan and sauté the onion, garlic and chilies for 5 minutes, or until softened. Add the spices and sauté gently for a further 5 minutes, stirring occasionally.

Add the canned tomatoes, tomato paste, water and lemon juice, and bring to a boil. Reduce the heat and simmer for 15 minutes.

Add the fish and continue cooking for 10 minutes, or until the fish is cooked through and flakes easily. Stir in the chopped cilantro and serve with freshly cooked rice and accompaniments.

SQUID *with* HOT-PEPPER SAUCE

Prepare the squid by cutting off the tentacles and rinsing. Remove the discard the head, innards and central transparent quill. Rub off the purplish outer skin, rinse and slice.

Put the shallots, garlic and both types of chilies into a mortar and pestle and grind to a paste.

Heat the oil in a wok or large pan and gently sauté the paste for 3 minutes. Add the tomatoes, lime juice and sugar, and cook for 10 to 12 minutes, or until a thick sauce is formed.

Add the oregano, reserving a little for garnish, and squid, and simmer for 5 minutes, or until the squid is tender. Take care not to overcook, otherwise the squid will become rubbery. Serve sprinkled with the remaining oregano. If liked, Hot-Pepper Sauce (page 10) can be added to increase the heat intensity.

Squid with Hot-Pepper Sauce ▶

HEAT 4

Serves 4

1½ lb assorted white fish, such as
    monkfish, cod and sole, cleaned and
    filleted

1 cup lime juice

3 tbsp olive or sunflower oil

2 onions, thinly sliced

2 garlic cloves, crushed

4 green de agua chilies, seeded and
    sliced

4 tomatoes, peeled, seeded and
    chopped

salt and pepper

dash of hot-pepper sauce

2 tbsp freshly chopped cilantro

shredded crisp lettuce

freshly chopped cilantro, green pitted
    olives and lime wedges, to garnish

warm pita bread or crusty bread, to
    serve

HEAT 4–5

Serves 4

1 tbsp corn or sunflower oil

1 onion, finely chopped

1 garlic clove, crushed

2 green New Mexico chilies, seeded
    and finely chopped

2 cooked crabs, inedible parts
    discarded and flaked, or 12 oz
    flaked white crabmeat

1 cup fresh white bread crumbs

⅓ cup whole kernel corn

2 large eggs, hard-boiled, shelled and
    finely chopped

salt and pepper

1 tbsp freshly chopped parsley

grated peel of 1 lime

lime twists and fresh herbs, to garnish

◀ Cebiche

CEBICHE

A traditional Mexican dish, sometimes spelt seviche or, in Spain, escabèche. It can be made with just shellfish or a mixture of white and shellfish. The fish must be absolutely fresh.

❧ Remove any bones from the fish, rinse and pat dry with paper towels. Cut into small bite-sized pieces and place in a shallow glass dish.

❧ Pour the lime juice over, ensuring that the fish is completely covered with the juice; if necessary add extra juice. Stir, then cover the dish and leave in the refrigerator to marinate for 10 to 12 hours. Stir occasionally during this time. The fish is ready when the flesh is firm in texture and white.

❧ Drain the juice from the fish and reserve the fish. Mix the remaining ingredients together, except the lettuce and garnishes. Stir in the drained fish.

❧ Place the lettuce in a serving bowl and arrange the fish and sauce on top. Garnish and serve with warm pita bread or crusty bread.

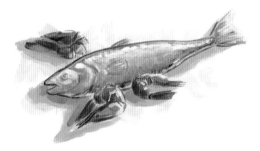

MEXICAN CRAB

Jaiba Mexicana

❧ Preheat the oven to 350°F.

❧ Heat the oil in a large pan and gently sauté the onion, garlic and chilies for 5 minutes, or until softened. Remove from the heat and stir in the crabmeat.

❧ Stir in half the bread crumbs, the corn kernels, chopped egg, seasoning to taste, parsley and lime peel. Mix together well.

❧ Divide the mixture between 4 cleaned crab shells or individual ovenproof dishes and sprinkle with the remaining bread crumbs. Bake for 20 minutes, or until thoroughly heated through. Garnish with lime twists and fresh herbs.

HEAT 4–5

Serves 4

Salsa

6 oz ripe tomatoes, peeled and seeded

2 shallots, finely chopped

2 green de agua chilies, roasted,
  peeled, seeded and finely chopped

1 small green bell pepper, roasted,
  peeled, seeded and finely chopped

1 to 2 tsp molasses sugar

1 small ripe papaya, peeled, pit
  removed and finely chopped

Tuna

4 tuna steaks, about 6 oz each

2 tbsp olive oil

juice of 2 limes

salt and pepper

fresh flat-leafed parsley, to garnish

freshly toasted bread, such as ciabatta,
  drizzled with olive oil, to serve

BROILED TUNA
with PAPAYA SALSA

Mix the salsa ingredients together. Put into a bowl, cover and leave for at least 1 hour for the flavors to develop.

Preheat the broiler to medium and line the broiler rack with foil. Wipe the tuna steaks and pat dry with paper towels. Mix the oil and lime juice with seasoning to taste and brush over both sides of the tuna steaks.

Place the fish on the foil-lined rack and broil for 2 minutes on each side. Reduce the heat and broil for a further 3 minutes on each side, or until the fish is tender and flakes easily. Serve on the toasted bread with the salsa. Garnish with parsley and lemon wedges.

HEAT 5–6

Serves 4

1 lb fish fillets, such as mackerel, sea
  bream, bass or pollack

1 tbsp corn or sunflower oil

1 large onion, sliced

5 red serrano chilies, seeded and sliced
  thinly

1 tsp ground ginger

1 tsp ground cinnamon

1 tsp ground cumin

3 carrots, sliced

4½ cups peeled and thickly sliced
  potatoes

2½ cups fish or vegetable stock

2 zucchini, trimmed and sliced

salt and pepper

4 oz raw shrimp, shelled

2 tbsp freshly chopped tarragon

warm bread, to serve

SPICY FISH STEW

Remove any bones from the fish, then rinse and pat dry with paper towels. Cut into small cubes.

Heat the oil in a large pan and sauté the onion and chilies for 5 minutes. Add the spices and cook for a further 3 minutes.

Add the carrots, potatoes and stock. Bring to a boil, cover the pan, reduce the heat and simmer gently for 15 minutes, or until the potatoes are beginning to break down.

Add the zucchini, cubed fish and the shrimp, and cook for 5 to 8 minutes, or until the vegetables and fish are cooked. Season to taste and stir in the chopped tarragon. Serve in deep bowls with warm bread.

Broiled Tuna with Papaya Salsa ▶

RED MULLET *with* TOMATO COULIS

Serves 4

2 large red mullet or snappers, filleted
  and boned

4 tbsp olive oil

½ cup lime juice

2 green Anaheim chilies, deseeded and
  finely sliced

1 to 2 tsp Mexican honey, warmed

Tomato Coulis

1 tbsp olive oil

2 shallots, chopped

1 garlic clove, crushed

3 red Anaheim chilies, seeded and
  chopped

1 tbsp tomato paste

1 tbsp water

3 cups peeled, seeded and chopped
  ripe tomatoes

juice of ½ lemon

salt and pepper

lime wedges and grated lime peel, to
  garnish

Rinse the fish and pat dry with paper towels. Place in a shallow dish. Mix the oil, lime juice, chilies and honey together and pour over the fish. Cover and leave to marinate for at least 1 hour. Turn occasionally during this time.

Meanwhile, make the coulis. Heat the oil in a pan and sauté the shallots, garlic and chilies for 5 minutes, or until softened. Blend the tomato paste with the water and add to the pan, together with the chopped tomatoes, lime juice and seasoning. Bring to a boil, cover the pan, reduce the heat and simmer for 15 minutes.

Remove from the heat and allow to cool slightly. Purée in a food processor, then pass through a fine strainer to remove any seeds. Check the seasoning and heat gently when required.

Preheat the broiler to medium and line the broiler rack with foil. Drain the fish and place on the foil-lined rack. Broil for 8 to 10 minutes, or until tender and the flesh flakes easily. Turn the fish once during broiling.

To serve, pour the tomato coulis onto 4 serving plates and place the cooked fish on top. Garnish with lime wedges and grated lime peel.

ORANGE- *and* CHILI-MARINATED SARDINES

HEAT 5

Serves 4

*8 to 12 fresh sardines (depending
   on size), cleaned*
½ cup orange juice
4 tbsp olive oil
*4 green jalapeño chilies, seeded and
   finely sliced*
1 tbsp soft brown sugar
few sprigs of fresh rosemary
*orange wedges and sprigs of fresh
   rosemary, to garnish*

Wipe or lightly rinse the sardines and pat dry with paper towels. Place in a shallow dish. Mix the orange juice, oil, chilies and sugar together and pour over the sardines. Tear the sprigs of rosemary into small pieces and scatter over the top. Cover and chill for at least 2 hours, turning the sardines occasionally.

Preheat the broiler to medium and line the broiler rack with foil. Drain the sardines and place on the foil-lined rack. Broil for 3 to 4 minutes, or until cooked through, basting with the marinade at least once during broiling. Garnish with orange wedges and sprigs of rosemary.

If liked, the sardines could be cooked on a barbecue for 3 to 4 minutes once the coals are ready. It is best to place them in a hinged fish rack.

YOGURT-SPICED FISH

HEAT 5

Serves 4

*4 haddock or cod steaks, about
   6 oz each*
1 tbsp corn or sunflower oil
*3 red jalapeño chilies, seeded and
   finely sliced*
2 garlic cloves, crushed
1 tsp turmeric
1 tsp ground cumin
1 tsp ground coriander
1 tsp ground fenugreek
6 cardamom pods, crushed
⅔ cup plain yogurt
2 tbsp flaked almonds, toasted
fresh herbs, to garnish

Lightly rinse the fish, cut into cubes and place in a shallow dish.

Heat the oil and gently sauté the garlic and chilies for 3 minutes, stirring frequently. Add the spices and cook gently for a further 3 to 4 minutes. Remove from the heat and stir in the yogurt. Pour over the fish, then cover and leave to marinate in the refrigerator for at least 1 hour, turning the fish over after 30 minutes.

Preheat the broiler to medium and line the broiler rack with foil. Drain the fish from the yogurt mixture and thread onto skewers. Broil for 3 to 4 minutes, or until tender and the fish flakes easily. Serve sprinkled with the almonds and garnished with fresh herbs.

Orange- and Chili - ▶
Marinated Sardines

BARBECUED JUMBO SHRIMP

HEAT 4-5

Serves 4

*1 lb raw jumbo shrimp, thawed if
frozen*
salad leaves and lime twists, to garnish

Marinade
grated peel and juice of 2 limes
*3 huachinango chilies, seeded and
sliced*
*2 lemongrass stalks, outer leaves
removed and sliced*
*2-inch piece gingerroot, peeled and
grated*
2 garlic cloves, crushed
1 tbsp honey, warmed
6 tbsp olive oil
1 tbsp freshly chopped cilantro

If using fresh shrimp, shell and devein them. Place in a shallow dish. Mix the marinade ingredients together and pour over the shrimp. Cover and leave to marinate for at least 4 hours, turning occasionally in the marinade.

Preheat the broiler to medium-hot or light the barbecue coals 20 minutes before required.

Have ready four long wooden skewers that have been soaked in cold water for 1 hour.

Drain the shrimp and reserve a little of the marinade. Thread the shrimp onto the skewers and brush with the marinade.

Cook under the broiler, or on the barbecue, turning at least once, for 5 minutes, or until the shrimp turn pink. Serve garnished with salad leaves and lime twists.

SCALLOPS *with* HABANERO *and* MANGO SALSA

HEAT 8–9

Serves 4

Salsa
*1 small ripe mango, peeled, seed
removed and finely chopped*
*3 scallions, trimmed and finely
chopped*
*2 orange habanero chilies, seeded and
chopped*
*2-inch piece cucumber, seeded and
finely diced*
*2 tomatoes, peeled, seeded and finely
chopped*
*1 to 2 tsp dark brown or molasses
sugar*
2 tbsp freshly chopped chervil

Scallops
12 large fresh scallops, cleaned
4 tbsp unsalted butter
1 tbsp olive or sunflower oil
*assorted bitter salad leaves, such as
arugula, escarole, radicchio and
endive*
edible flowers, to garnish

Combine all the salsa ingredients together, put into a bowl and cover. Chill for 15 minutes and then use immediately.

Cut the scallops into thick slices. Rinse and thoroughly dry. Heat the butter and oil in a skillet. When the butter is bubbling slightly, add the scallops and cook gently for 2 to 3 minutes, or until just cooked. Drain.

Arrange the salad leaves on a serving platter or in a bowl and top with the scallops. Garnish with the edible flowers and serve with the salsa.

◀ *Barbecued Jumbo Shrimp*

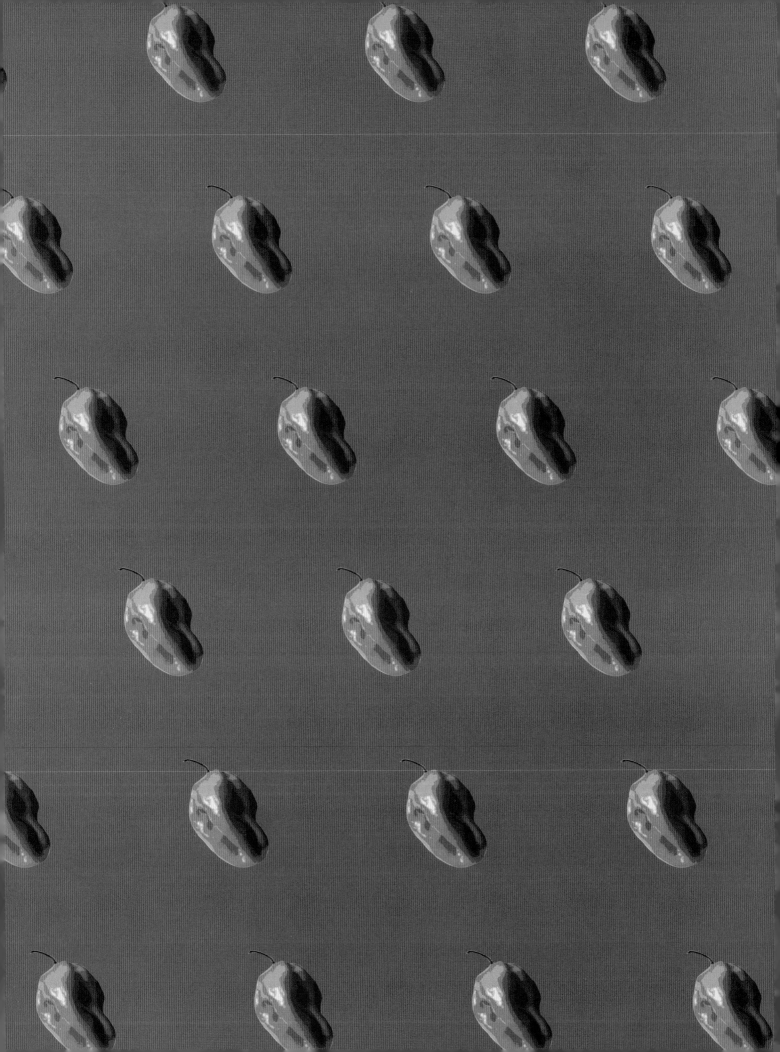

Chapter 6

Poultry

DUCK *in* GREEN CHILI SAUCE

HEAT 5

Serves 4

4 green serrano chilies, seeded and
sliced
1½ cups seeded and chopped
tomatillos or green tomatoes
1 onion, chopped
2 garlic cloves, chopped
grated peel of ½ lemon, if using green
tomatoes
⅔ cup chicken stock
2 tbsp freshly chopped cilantro
2 tsp honey
salt and pepper
1 tbsp arrowroot
1 tbsp water
4 duck breasts
Salsa Rojo (page 46), to serve
cilantro sprigs, to garnish

Tomatillos are a type of tomato with a zesty bitter flavor and have a papery husk around each fruit. When cooked they lose their bitterness but still retain their lemony tang. They can also be bought canned.

🌶 Preheat the broiler to medium-high.

🌶 Put the chilies, tomatillos or tomatoes, onion, garlic and lemon peel, if using, into a food processor and blend to form a purée. Push through a fine strainer into a pan and gradually stir in the stock.

🌶 Heat the chili mixture gently for 4 minutes, stirring occasionally. Then stir in the cilantro, honey and seasoning to taste.

Blend the arrowroot with the water, stir into the pan and cook, stirring constantly, until the sauce thickens and clears. Keep warm.

🌶 Wipe the duck breasts, discard any excess fat and prick the skin with a fork. Season with salt and pepper.

🌶 Place the duck breasts, skin side uppermost, in a broiler pan and broil, turning at least once, for 25 minutes, or until cooked to personal preference.

🌶 To serve, pour a little of the chili sauce onto each serving plate and slice the duck breasts. Arrange in a fan shape with the Salsa Rojo and serve extra sauce separately. Garnish with cilantro sprigs.

CHILI-CHICKEN *with* PINE NUTS

HEAT 6

Serves 4

1 tbsp sunflower oil
1 tbsp butter
4 chicken portions
4 oz lean slab bacon, trimmed and
   cubed
1 onion, sliced
1 garlic clove, crushed
4 green fresno chilies, seeded and
   sliced
¼ cup all-purpose flour
2 cups chicken stock
grated peel of 1 lemon
salt and pepper
⅔ cup whole-kernel corn
2 tbsp freshly chopped parsley
3 tbsp pine nuts, toasted

🌶 Preheat the oven to 375°F.

🌶 Heat the oil and butter in a skillet and seal the chicken portions and bacon on all sides. Drain and place in a large ovenproof casserole.

🌶 Add the onion, garlic and chilies to the skillet and gently sauté for 5 minutes, or until softened. Sprinkle in the flour and cook, stirring constantly for 2 minutes. Gradually add the stock, then bring to a boil. Add the lemon peel with seasoning to taste.

🌶 Pour the onion mixture over the chicken, cover the casserole and cook for 40 minutes. Remove from the oven and stir in the corn. Cook for a further 15 minutes or until the chicken portions are cooked through and the juices run clear. Stir in the parsley and pine nuts, and serve.

Duck in Green Chili Sauce ▶

CHICKEN STRIPS *with* NUOC CHAM

HEAT 7

Serves 4

10 oz boneless chicken breast, skinned

Marinade

2 shallots, finely chopped

1 garlic clove, crushed

4 Thai red chilies, seeded and chopped

2-inch piece gingerroot, peeled and grated

2 tbsp soy sauce

2 tsp honey, warmed

2 tbsp lemon juice

chopped chili, to garnish

Nuoc Cham

1 Thai red chili, seeded and finely chopped

1 tbsp lime juice

¼ cup Thai fish sauce

1 tbsp roasted peanuts, finely crushed

2 scallions, trimmed and finely shredded

Nuoc Cham *is a traditional Vietnamese dipping sauce served at the table to season dishes. The sauce can also be stirred into soups and rice dishes, or poured over fish and meat dishes.*

✎ Cut the chicken breasts into narrow strips, about 3 x ½ inch, and place in a shallow dish. Combine all the marinade ingredients together and pour over the chicken strips. Turn to ensure they are well coated. Cover the dish and chill for at least 3 hours, turning the chicken occasionally in the marinade.

✎ Preheat the broiler to medium-high.

✎ Drain the chicken and thread onto wooden skewers that have been soaked in cold water for 1 hour.

✎ Meanwhile, prepare the *Nuoc Cham* sauce. Put all the ingredients into a small pan and heat through, stirring occasionally. Reserve.

✎ Brush the chicken strips with a little of the marinade and broil, brushing occasionally with the marinade and turning the strips, for 8 to 10 minutes, or until tender and the juices run clear. Serve with the sauce, garnished with the chopped chili.

TAMALE PIE

HEAT 7

Serves 6

3 tbsp sunflower or olive oil

¼ cup all-purpose flour

5 ancho dried chilies, roasted and
   rehydrated (page 16)

1 garlic clove, crushed

3 shallots, chopped

2 tbsp tomato paste

1 cup chicken stock

1 tbsp freshly chopped oregano

12 oz cooked chicken meat, cut into
   thin strips

⅔ cup whole-kernel corn

4½ cups water

2 cups cornmeal or polenta

2 tsp chili powder

1 to 2 tsp salt

1 tsp pepper

2 tbsp olive oil

Salsa Rojo (page 46) and green
   salad, to serve

This is one of Mexico's oldest dishes, dating back to Aztec times and traditionally served at festivals and feast days. It is rather like a stuffed dumpling – the dough is wrapped in corn husks, then steamed and served with a salsa or mole sauce.

Heat the sunflower or olive oil in a pan, add the flour and cook, very gently, stirring frequently, for 8 to 10 minutes, or until browned. Take great care not to burn the mixture.

Chop the rehydrated chilies and add to the flour mixture with the garlic, shallots, tomato paste blended with the stock, and the oregano. Bring to a boil, then reduce the heat and simmer for 15 minutes. Add the chicken and corn, mix well and set aside until cool.

Bring the water to just below boiling point, then take off the heat and gradually stir in the cornmeal or polenta, chili powder, salt and pepper in a thin, steady stream. Stir until smooth, then return to a medium heat and simmer for 5 to 10 minutes, stirring occasionally.

Preheat the oven to 350°F.

Spread half the cornmeal or polenta mixture in the bottom of a lightly oiled 8-inch oblong baking dish and place the cooled chicken mixture on top. Cover with the remaining cornmeal mixture. Drizzle with the 2 tbsp of olive oil. Bake for about 1 hour, or until the top is golden brown. Serve cut into wedges with Salsa Rojo and green salad.

TURKEY *with* SMOKED CHILI BARBECUE SAUCE

HEAT 5

Serves 4

½ cup white-wine vinegar

½ tsp ground cloves

1 tsp ground cinnamon

2 tsp juniper berries, crushed

4 tbsp olive or sunflower oil

1 onion, chopped

3 garlic cloves, crushed

½ cup dark brown sugar

6 smoked dried chilies, such as Pasilla
   de Oaxaco or Chipotle Grande,
   roasted, rehydrated (page 16) and
   chopped

2 tbsp tomato paste

⅔ cup water

1 tsp Worcestershire sauce

8 turkey thighs

sliced starfruit and salad leaves, to
   garnish

rice salad, to serve

Most barbecue sauces are made with cayenne and other hot chilies. The use of dried chilies in this sauce gives it a roundness or smoothness that you would not get with just fresh chilies. If, however, dried are unavailable, fresno chilies will make a delicious and appetizing sauce.

Put the vinegar in a pan with the spices and bring to a boil. Boil for 3 minutes and set aside.

Heat the oil in a skillet and sauté the onion and garlic for 5 minutes, or until softened. Add the sugar and boil for 3 minutes. Then stir in the vinegar mixture, chopped chilies, tomato paste, water and Worcestershire sauce. Cook over gentle heat for about 30 minutes and allow to cool slightly before using.

Place the turkey thighs in a shallow baking dish and pour the sauce over. Cover the dish and leave to chill for at least 2 hours, turning the turkey at least once during the marinading.

Preheat the broiler to medium.

Drain the turkey and place on the foil-lined broiler rack. Brush with a little of the marinade. Broil for 12 to 15 minutes, brushing with the marinade and turning occasionally, until the turkey is cooked. Serve, garnished with sliced starfruit, salad leaves and a rice salad.

*Turkey with Smoked Chili ▶
Barbecue Sauce*

ARROZ CON POLLO

HEAT 5

Serves 4

3 tbsp olive or sunflower oil

4 chicken portions, cut in half

1 Spanish onion, chopped

2 garlic cloves, crushed

*5 red Anaheim chilies, seeded and
    sliced*

heaped 2 cups risotto rice

few strands of saffron

2½ to 3¼ cups chicken stock

salt and pepper

4 oz raw shelled shrimp

⅔ cup shelled peas

4 oz green beans, trimmed and sliced

*1 lb fresh mussels, scrubbed, beards
    removed and any open ones
    discarded*

*lemon wedges and flat-leafed parsley,
    to garnish*

*If using cooked shrimp, add at the end of
cooking time when the chicken is cooked and
heat through for just 2 to 3 minutes.*

➴ Heat the oil in a paella or large skillet and
brown the chicken on all sides. Remove from
the pan and drain on paper towels.

➴ Add the onion, garlic and chilies to the pan
and sauté for 5 minutes. Add the rice and
saffron, and cook, stirring occasionally for a
further 3 minutes.

➴ Return the chicken to the pan and stir in 2
cups of the stock and seasoning. Bring to a
boil, then simmer for 20 minutes, adding more
stock as necessary.

➴ Add the shrimp, vegetables and mussels to
the pan with extra stock as required and cook
for a further 8 to 10 minutes, or until the rice
is tender and the chicken juices run clear.
Discard any mussels that have not opened.
Season to taste and serve garnished with lemon
wedges and parsley.

SIZZLING CHICKEN FAJITAS

HEAT 4

Serves 4

2 tbsp sunflower oil

*8 oz boneless chicken breast, cut into
    thin strips*

1 onion, cut into wedges

2 garlic cloves

4 red fresno chilies, seeded and sliced

*1 red bell pepper, seeded and cut into
    strips*

*1 green bell pepper, seeded and cut
    into strips*

2 zucchini, trimmed and cut into strips

8 wheat tortillas, warmed

⅔ cup sour cream

Guacamole (page 29)

*1 bunch scallions, trimmed and cut
    into strips*

*3-inch piece cucumber, trimmed and
    cut into thin strips*

*Ready-made fajitas marinades are available
but it is well worth making your own as you
can then vary the flavor according to the
ingredients you use. Fajitas can be made from
seafood, pork and just vegetables, as well as
beef and chicken. They are best served in
warm tortillas with spicy salsas and
sour cream.*

➴ Heat the oil in a heavy-bottomed pan and
cook the chicken strips over high heat, stirring
constantly, for 5 minutes, or until cooked.
Drain and reserve.

➴ Add the onion, garlic and chilies to the
oil in the pan over high heat for 2 minutes.
Add the bell peppers and zucchini, and cook
over high heat for 4 minutes, or until the
vegetables have begun to blacken very
slightly at the edges.

➴ Return the chicken to the pan and heat
until piping hot. Serve immediately. Spread
a warmed tortilla with sour cream and
Guacamole, top with some chicken and
vegetable mixture, scallions and cucumber.
Roll up and eat.

◄ *Arroz con Pollo*

TURKEY *in* CHOCOLATE SAUCE

Mole Poblano

Serves 4

3 dried ancho chilies

3 dried pasilla chilies

3 dried mulato chilies

1 onion, sliced

2 garlic cloves, crushed

2 tbsp sesame seeds, toasted

2 tbsp blanched almonds, cut into
   slivers and toasted

1 tsp ground coriander

½ tsp freshly ground black pepper

few cloves

3 to 4 tbsp sunflower oil

1¼ cups chicken stock

3 cups peeled, seeded and chopped
   tomatoes

2 tsp ground cinnamon

⅓ cup raisins

½ cup pumpkin seeds, toasted

2 oz unsweetened chocolate, melted

1 tbsp red-wine vinegar

8 turkey thigh portions or 2 boneless
   chicken breasts

extra sesame seeds, toasted, and
   fresh herbs, to garnish

To many the idea of adding chocolate to a savory dish may seem a little strange but Mexican chocolate is bitter, not at all like most chocolate we know. Use the darkest unsweetened chocolate you can find. Chicken is everyday fare in Mexico, while turkey is kept for festivals and special occasions. If the dried chilies are unavailable, substitute the darkest chili powder you can find.

🌶 Roast the dried chilies and rehydrate as described on page 16, then put into a food processor or a mortar and pestle with the onion, garlic, sesame seeds, almonds, coriander, black pepper and cloves. Grind to form a paste.

🌶 Heat 2 tbsp of the oil in a heavy-bottomed pan and gently sauté the paste for 5 minutes, stirring frequently.

🌶 Add ⅔ cup of the stock, the tomatoes, cinnamon, raisins and pumpkin seeds. Bring to a boil, then reduce the heat and simmer for 15 minutes, or until a thick consistency is reached. Stir in the melted chcolate and vinegar, mixing together well, cover, keep warm and reserve.

🌶 Meanwhile, heat the remaining oil in a skillet and seal the turkey thighs or chicken breasts on all sides. Drain off the oil and add the remaining stock. Bring to a boil, then reduce the heat and simmer for 15 minutes, or until tender. Drain off any liquid.

🌶 Pour the sauce over the turkey or chicken and reheat gently. Serve garnished with toasted sesame seeds and fresh herbs.

Turkey in Chocolate Sauce ▶

BARBECUED CHICKEN WINGS

HEAT 5

Serves 4

12 to 16 chicken wings
Salsa Verde (page 47), tossed green
   salad and warm bread, to serve

Marinade
2 tbsp sunflower oil
2 tbsp dark soft brown sugar
2 tbsp soy sauce
½ cup orange juice
2 garlic cloves, crushed
4 red jalapeño chilies, seeded and
   sliced

➤ Wipe the chicken wings and trim if necessary. Place in a large, shallow dish.

➤ Mix all the marinade ingredients together in a pan and heat through, stirring occasionally, until the sugar has dissolved. Bring to a boil and boil for 5 minutes. Allow to cool slightly, then pour over the chicken wings. Turn the wings to ensure they are well coated, then cover the dish and leave in a cool place for at least 3 hours. Turn the wings or spoon the marinade over the chicken occasionally.

➤ Preheat the broiler to medium-low. Alternatively, light barbecue coals 20 minutes before cooking.

➤ Drain the chicken wings, reserving a little of the marinade, and thread onto wooden skewers that have been soaked in cold water for 1 hour. Place on the broiler rack lined with foil or over the barbecue coals and brush with the reserved marinade. Cook, turning occasionally and brushing with the reserved marinade, for 10 to 12 minutes, or until the wings are cooked. Serve with the Salsa Verde, salad and bread.

TURKEY TAMALES

HEAT 5

Serves 4

Tamales
8 dried corn husks
¾ cup plus 2 tbsp vegetable fat or lard
1 lb masa harina or polenta, sifted
1 tsp baking powder
1 tsp salt
about 2 cups chicken stock, warmed

Filling
2 tbsp sunflower oil
1 onion, chopped
3 garlic cloves, crushed
5 red de agua chilies, seeded and
   chopped
1 small red bell pepper, seeded and
   chopped
1 small green bell pepper, seeded and
   chopped
2 tbsp tomato paste
2 tbsp water
½ cup whole-kernel corn
salt and pepper
2 tbsp chopped oregano
10 oz cooked turkey meat, shredded
   or ground
Salsa Verde (page 47), to serve
fresh herbs, to garnish

Masa harina is a corn flour used for making corn tortillas. The corn is treated by being boiled in lime water for several hours, then drained and dried. The outer skin is removed and the kernels ground into cornmeal. If unavailable, use polenta or yellow cornmeal.

➤ Soak the corn husks overnight in warm water.

➤ Cream the fat until soft and sift the dry ingredients together. Gradually beat the masa harina or polenta into the fat with a little of the stock after each addition, until a firm but pliable dough is formed. Chill while preparing the filling.

➤ Heat the oil in a skillet and sauté the onion, garlic and chilies for 5 minutes, or until softened. Add the red and green bell peppers and sauté for a further 3 minutes. Blend the

tomato paste with the water and pour into the pan with the remaining chicken stock. Bring to a boil and simmer for 5 minutes Add the corn, seasoning, oregano and turkey, and mix together well.

➤ Drain the corn husks (alternatively, you could use oblongs of foil) and place on the work surface. Form the chilled dough into rectangular shapes a little smaller than the corn husks or foil, and place on top of the husks or foil. Divide the filling between the husks or foil and fold the long side over to encase the filling.

➤ Place upright in a steamer over a pan of simmering water. Cover the steamer with a lid and steam for 1 hour, refilling the pan with boiling water as necessary. Serve with Salsa Verde, garnished with fresh herbs.

◄ *Barbecued Chicken Wings*

VIETNAMESE BROILED CHICKEN

HEAT 5–7

Serves 4

6 dried ancho chilies, roasted,
   rehydrated (page 16) and seeded
2 lemongrass stalks chopped, outer
   leaves removed
2 garlic cloves, crushed
2-inch piece gingerroot, peeled and
   grated
1 heaped cup chopped onions
1 tbsp dark brown sugar
1 tsp turmeric
2 tbsp sunflower oil
4 chicken portions, cut in half
flat-leafed parsley, lemon wedges and
   sliced green chilies, to garnish

If preferred, bird's eye (Thai) chilies can be substituted for the dried chilies. Depending on your heat tolerance, you should use 1–3 bird's eye (Thai) chilies instead of the dried ancho chilies.

🌶 Put the chilies into a food processor with the lemongrass, garlic, ginger, onions, sugar and turmeric. Blend to form a thick, chunky paste.

🌶 Heat the oil in a skillet and sauté the paste, stirring constantly, for 2 minutes. Remove from the heat, allow to cool slightly and brush over the chicken portions. Cover the chicken and leave in a cool place for at least 3 hours.

🌶 Preheat the broiler to medium-high.

🌶 Place the chicken on the broiler rack lined with foil and broil, turning occasionally, for 15 minutes, or until the chicken is tender and the juices run clear. Serve garnished with flat-leafed parsley, lemon wedges and slices of green chilies.

DUCK BREASTS
with PIPIAN VERDE

HEAT 5

Serves 4

Pipián Verde
⅓ cup pumpkin seeds, toasted
2 tbsp sunflower oil
1 small onion, chopped
3 or 4 green fresno chilies, seeded and
   chopped
2 garlic cloves, chopped
⅔ cup chicken stock
1 tbsp freshly chopped cilantro
¼ tsp salt
2 cups prepared and chopped fresh
   spinach leaves

4 duck breasts, about 6 oz each

This sauce contains pumpkin seeds which are used to thicken and flavor. Mexicans also use sesame seeds and pine nuts for the same purpose. Toasted pumpkin seeds can also be used as appetizers with drinks.

🌶 Reserve a few of the pumpkin seeds for garnish and finely grind the remainder.

🌶 Heat the oil in a pan and gently sauté the onion, chilies and garlic for 3 minutes. Add the stock and simmer for 1 minute. Add the ground pumpkin seeds, cilantro, salt and spinach to the pan and simmer for a further 3 minutes. Remove from the heat and keep warm.

🌶 Preheat the broiler to high.

🌶 Meanwhile, prick the skin on the duck breasts with a fork and place, skin-side uppermost, on the foil–lined broiler pan. Broil for 2 minutes, on both sides, then with skin sides uppermost, reduce the broiler to medium-hot and continue broiling, for 15 to 20 minutes, turning at least once, or according to personal preference. Serve the duck breasts, sprinkled with the reserved pumpkin seeds, with the Pipián Verde.

Vietnamese Broiled Chicken ▶

ROASTED DUCK *with* CHILI

HEAT 4-5

Serves 4

1 4-lb oven-ready duck
4 red serrano chilies, seeded and
  finely chopped
2 tbsp dark brown sugar
1 tsp salt
1 tsp ground cinnamon
½ tsp ground cloves
grated peel of 1 lime
grated lime peel and flat-leafed
  parsley, to garnish

Salsa

1½ cups peeled, seeded and finely
  chopped ripe tomatoes
6 scallions, trimmed and finely
  chopped
1 Grenadillo, halved, with seeds
  removed
2 red serrano chilies, seeded and finely
  chopped

🌶 Wipe the duck, inside and out, discarding any excess fat from the cavity. Prick the skin all over with a fork. Mix the chilies, sugar, salt, cinnamon, cloves and lime peel together. Sprinkle the inside of the duck with 1 tbsp of the mixture and use the remainder to rub all over the duck skin. Leave in a cool place for at least 4 hours.

🌶 Preheat the oven to 400°F 15 minutes before roasting the duck.

🌶 Place the duck on a trivet or rack standing in a roasting pan. Roast in the oven for 1¾ to 2 hours, or until the duck is tender and the juices run clear.

🌶 Meanwhile, make the Salsa. Combine all the ingredients and leave for at least 30 minutes to allow the flavors to develop. Serve with the cooked duck, garnished with lime peel and flat-leafed parsley.

CHICKEN *in* RED CHILI *and* TOMATO SAUCE

HEAT 7

Serves 4

2½ lb chicken
2 onions
1 carrot, roughly chopped
3 bay leaves
6 dried ancho chilies, roasted,
  rehydrated (page 16) and seeded
2 garlic cloves
4 tbsp sesame seeds, toasted
½ tsp ground cinnamon
½ tsp ground cloves
1 tbsp sunflower oil
14-oz can crushed tomatoes
1 tbsp tomato paste
1 tbsp freshly chopped oregano
salad and warm bread, to serve

When choosing tomatoes for Mexican dishes, look for the large beef tomatoes as they are the nearest thing to Mexican tomatoes. Canned tomatoes can be used instead, but you may need to reduce the liquid in the recipe.

🌶 Rinse the chicken and place in a large pan with one of the onions, the carrot and bay leaves. Cover with cold water and bring to a boil. Skim off any foam that rises to the surface. Cover the pan with a lid and simmer for 1½ hours, or until tender and the juices run clear.

🌶 Allow to cool, then remove the cooked chicken meat from the carcase, discarding the skin, and cut into thin strips. Reserve 1¼ cups of the cooking liquid.

🌶 Put the rehydrated chilies into a food processor with the remaining onion (chopped), the garlic, sesame seeds and spices. Blend with a little of the reserved stock to make a smooth paste.

🌶 Heat the oil in a skillet and sauté the paste gently for 2 minutes. Add the chopped tomatoes, tomato paste and remaining stock. Bring to a boil, reduce the heat and simmer for 10 minutes.

🌶 Add the chicken to the pan and simmer for a further 10 to 15 minutes, or until the chicken is piping hot. Serve, sprinkled with the chopped oregano, with salad and warm bread.

Roasted Duck with Chili ▶

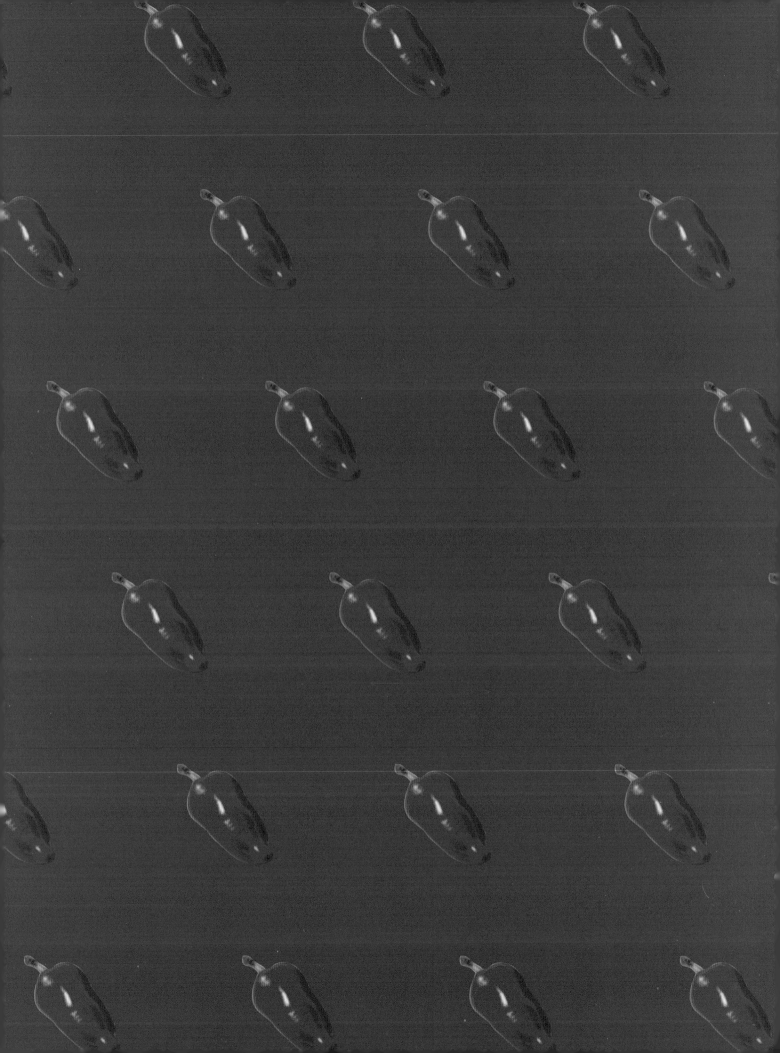

Chapter 7

Meat

HEAT 7-8

Serves 4

1 tbsp sunflower oil

1 large onion, chopped

2 garlic cloves, crushed

3 rocotillo chilies, seeded and sliced

12 oz ground beef

1 green bell pepper, seeded and
    chopped

1 tsp paprika

14-oz can crushed tomatoes

⅔ cup beef stock

1 tsp sugar

salt and pepper

14-oz can pinto or red kidney
    beans, drained and rinsed

2 tsp red-wine vinegar

1 tbsp freshly chopped oregano

freshly cooked rice and sour cream, to
    serve

HEAT 3-4

Serves 4

3 tbsp sunflower oil or ghee

1 onion, chopped

2 garlic cloves, peeled and crushed

1-inch piece gingerroot, peeled and
    grated

3 or 4 red Anaheim chilies, seeded and
    sliced

6 green cardamom pods

1 tsp ground coriander

1 tsp ground cumin

½ tsp ground cloves

1½ lb braising steak, trimmed and
    cubed

juice of 1 lemon

2 tbsp tomato paste

3 tbsp water

3 cups beef stock

⅔ cup plain yogurt

2 tbsp ground almonds

1 cup basmati rice

few strands of saffron

1 hard-boiled egg, shelled and sliced

1 tbsp pistachio nuts, chopped

CHILI CON CARNE

Perhaps the best-known Mexican dish of which there are many variations, this is sometimes served with refried beans as well as rice. The sour cream helps to offset the fire from the chilies.

Heat the oil in a large pan and sauté the onion, garlic and chilies for 5 minutes, or until softened. Add the beef and cook, stirring constantly, for 5 to 8 minutes, or until the beef is browned and separate.

Add the green bell pepper and cook for 3 minutes. Then add paprika and cook for 1 minute. Add the crushed tomatoes, stock and sugar with seasoning to taste and bring to a boil. Reduce the heat and simmer for 20 minutes. Then add the drained beans and vinegar, and simmer for 10 minutes, or until the beef is cooked. Stir in the oregano and serve with the rice and sour cream.

BIRIANI

Birianis were developed by the Moghul chefs who cooked for the Indian emperors. The classic method is to part-cook the rice and filling, then layer them and continue their cooking. A rich and attractive dish which needs no other accompaniments except for a couple of pickles or chutneys.

Heat the oil or ghee in a large pan and sauté the onion, garlic, ginger and chilies for 5 minutes. Add the remaining spices and sauté for a further 3 minutes. Using a slotted spoon, remove the onion mixture from the pan and reserve.

Add half the beef to the pan and sauté for 5 minutes, or until sealed, stirring frequently. Drain and reserve. Repeat with the remaining beef. Then return the onion mixture and both batches of sealed beef to the pan.

Add the lemon juice and tomato paste blended with the water, and the stock. Bring to a boil, cover the pan, then reduce the heat and simmer gently for 1 hour, stirring occasionally. Stir in the yogurt and ground almonds.

Meanwhile, cook the rice for 10 minutes with the saffron threads in lightly salted water. Drain and reserve.

Preheat the oven to 350°F.

Place half the rice in the bottom of a baking dish or casserole and cover with the beef mixture. Spoon the remaining rice on top and cover with a lid or foil. Cook in the oven for about 40 minutes, or until the beef is tender. Serve garnished with the hard-boiled egg and pistachio nuts.

EMPANADAS

Serves 6

3 oz ground pork

3 oz ground beef

1 small onion, finely chopped

2 Scotch bonnet chilies, seeded and
   finely chopped

½ small red bell pepper, seeded and
   finely chopped

½ small green bell pepper, seeded and
   finely chopped

½ tsp ground cloves

1 tsp ground cinnamon

1 tbsp tomato paste

5 tbsp water

1 tsp clear honey

juice of 1 lime

1½ lb prepared piecrust dough

oil for deep-frying

Red or Green Chili Sauce (page 47)

Empanadas are little filled pastry turnovers that are either deep fried or baked. The filling can be sweet or savory. In Mexico these are sold on stalls in the street and usually served with a red or green chili sauce.

➧ Put the pork and beef into a nonstick skillet and fry over a gentle heat, stirring constantly, for 8 minutes, or until the meat has browned. Use the spoon to break up any lumps.

➧ Add the onion and chilies, and cook for 5 minutes, stirring frequently. Add both the bell peppers and spices, and cook for a further 3 minutes. Blend the tomato paste with the water and add to the pan, together with the honey and lime juice. Bring to a boil, then simmer for 15 minutes, stirring frequently, or until most of the liquid has evaporated. Allow to cool.

➧ Roll out the dough on a lightly floured surface and cut out 12 4-inch circles. Divide the filling between the dough circles, brush the edges with water and fold over to make small crescents. Pinch the edges together firmly.

➧ Heat the oil to 350°F and fry the Empanadas, a few at a time, for 3 minutes or until golden brown. Drain on paper towels and serve with Red or Green Chili Sauce.

HOT-*and*-SOUR BEEF FONDUE

Serves 4

1¼ cups good-quality beef stock

4 star anise

few cloves

few peppercorns

2-inch piece gingerroot, peeled
    and chopped

I onion, sliced

I garlic clove, sliced

3 Thai green chilies, seeded and sliced

3 tbsp red-wine vinegar

I tbsp honey

12 oz beef tenderloin, trimmed and
    sliced into thin strips

I red bell pepper, seeded and cut into
    strips

I yellow bell pepper, seeded and cut
    into strips

2 zucchini, trimmed and cut into strips

I fresh pineapple, peeled, cored and
    cut into small wedges

1½ cups bean sprouts

Sauce

I tbsp soy sauce

2 tsp fish sauce

I tsp honey, warmed

I Thai red chili, seeded and sliced

This recipe is based on the Mongolian Hot Pot which is a version of a cheese fondue or the French beef fondue. The food is cooked in the hot stock which is then drunk at the end of the meal to clear the palate.

❧ Put the stock into a pan with the spices, ginger, onion, garlic and chilies. Bring to a boil and simmer for 10 minutes, then add the vinegar and honey. Pour into a fondue pot placed over a burner and keep warm.

❧ Put the beef, peppers, zucchini and pineapple wedges into individual serving bowls.

❧ Combine the sauce ingredients and pour into small dishes.

❧ To serve, spear the beef or vegetables onto skewers and dip into the hot stock for 1 to 2 minutes, or until cooked to personal preference. Dip into the sauce before eating.

❧ When all the beef, vegetables and fruit have been eaten, add the bean sprouts to the fondue pot and heat through for 1 to 2 minutes. Ladle into soup bowls and drink to clear the palate.

LAMB *in* SPICY YOGURT SAUCE

HEAT 3-4

Serves 4

2 tbsp sunflower or olive oil
4 lean boneless lamb steaks, about
   5 oz each
1 onion, sliced
2 garlic cloves, crushed
3 green New Mexico chilies, peeled,
   seeded and sliced
1 tsp ground cumin
½ tsp ground cloves
1 tsp ground cinnamon
12 green cardamom pods
1 cup water
1¼ cups plain yogurt
2 tbsp ground almonds
2 tbsp flaked almonds, toasted
flat-leafed parsley, to garnish

Heat the oil in a skillet and seal the lamb on both sides. Drain on paper towels and reserve.

Add the onion, garlic and chilies to the pan and sauté for 5 minutes, or until soft. Stir in the spices and cook for a further 3 minutes. Add the water to the pan and bring to a boil. Reduce the heat and add the lamb, then simmer for 10 minutes.

Stir the yogurt and ground almonds into the pan and cook for a further 15 minutes, or until the lamb is tender. Stir frequently during this time. (If the sauce is thickening too much, add a little extra water.)

Sprinkle the lamb and sauce with the flaked almonds and garnish with parsley.

LAMB TIKKA

HEAT 7-8

Serves 4

1 lb lean boneless lamb, trimmed
⅔ cup plain yogurt
2 tbsp tandoori paste
1 tsp ground coriander
1 tsp ground cumin
1 tsp turmeric
1 tsp ground ginger
3 garlic cloves, crushed
grated peel of 1 lemon
6 green serrano chilies, seeded and
   finely chopped
2 tbsp freshly chopped mint
8 baby onions
2 zucchini, trimmed and cut into
   1½-inch chunks
2 red bell peppers, seeded and cut
   into wedges
lemon wedges, to garnish

The correct way to cook a tikka dish is in a tandoori oven but as these are not readily available, broiling or barbecuing works just as well. The longer the meat is marinated, the better the flavor.

Cut the lamb into 1½-inch cubes and place in a shallow dish. Put the yogurt into a bowl and mix in the tandoori paste, spices, garlic, lemon peel, chilies and 1 tbsp of the mint. Spoon the marinade over the lamb, cover and chill for at least 4 hours, turning occasionally.

Preheat the broiler to medium-hot just before cooking.

Thread the lamb alternately with the prepared vegetables onto kebab skewers and broil for 10 to 15 minutes, or until cooked as preferred. Brush with the marinade during cooking. Serve sprinkled with the remaining chopped mint and lemon wedges.

KASHMIR LAMB

Serves 4

3 tbsp sunflower oil or ghee

1 large onion, sliced

2 garlic cloves

2 or 3 New Mexico red chilies, seeded
and sliced

1-inch piece gingerroot, peeled and
grated

1 tsp ground cumin

1 tsp turmeric

1 tsp ratan jot or few drops of red
food coloring

1 lb lamb tenderloin, trimmed and
cubed

4 tomatoes, peeled, seeded and
chopped

2 cups lamb or vegetable stock

2 tbsp pistachio nuts

⅓ cup cashew nuts

2 tbsp golden raisins

1 tbsp freshly chopped cilantro

freshly cooked rice, to serve

Kashmir dishes are usually red in color and this is achieved by the use of **ratan jot,** *a red herb food coloring. Kashmir foods are normally very rich and creamy due to the use of the nuts grown in the area.*

➤ Heat the oil or ghee in a large pan and sauté the onion, garlic, chilies and ginger for 5 minutes. Add the spices and sauté for a further 3 minutes, then stir in the *ratan jot* or

food coloring. Add the lamb in two batches and cook for 5 minutes, or until sealed, stirring frequently.

➤ Add the tomatoes and stock, then bring to a boil. Cover with a lid, reduce the heat and simmer for 40 minutes, stirring occasionally.

➤ Add the nuts and golden raisins, and simmer for a further 15 minutes, or until the meat is tender. Stir in the cilantro and serve with freshly cooked rice.

HEAT 6

Serves 4

1 lb lean ground pork

3 lemongrass stalks, outer leaves discarded and minced

1 tbsp Red Chili Paste (page 47)

grated peel of 1 lime

3 tomatoes, peeled, seeded and finely chopped

1 tsp turmeric

2 tsp minced galangal, or peeled and minced gingerroot

1 garlic clove, minced

¼ tsp salt

oil for deep-frying

lime wedges and chili flowers (page 11), to garnish

HEAT 6

Serves 4

1½ lb Chinese spareribs

Marinade

4 Hontaka or Thai red chilies, seeded and chopped

1¼ cups chicken stock

juice of 2 limes

1 tbsp soy sauce

1 tbsp hoisin sauce

1 tbsp unrefined brown sugar

2 tbsp tomato paste

2 tsp Worcestershire sauce

1 tsp ground cinnamon

½ tsp ground cloves

6 scallions, trimmed and chopped

PORK *and* CHILI BALLS

❧ Put the pork, lemongrass, Red Chili Paste and lime peel into a bowl. Stir in the tomatoes, turmeric, galangal or ginger, garlic and salt. Mix together well.

❧ Using slightly wet hands, form the pork mixture into small balls about the size of an apricot. Chill, covered, for at least 30 minutes.

❧ Heat the oil to 350°F and fry the balls in batches for 5 to 6 minutes, or until golden. Drain on paper towels. Serve garnished with lime wedges and chili flowers.

HOT- *and* SPICY- BARBECUED SPARERIBS

A nice, thoughtful gesture is to provide some finger bowls filled with warm water and a slice of lemon and some paper towels so that diners can rinse their fingers after eating this dish.

❧ Cut the spare ribs into separate ribs if necessary and place in a shallow dish. Mix all the marinade ingredients, except the scallions, together in a pan and bring to a boil. Simmer for 2 minutes, allow to cool and then add the scallions.

❧ Pour the marinade over the ribs, turning them to ensure they are well covered. Cover the dish and leave in the refrigerator to marinate for at least 4 hours, turning occasionally and spooning the marinade over.

❧ Preheat the oven to 375°F.

❧ Drain the ribs and place on a rack in a roasting pan with a little water in the bottom. Brush the ribs with the marinade and turn occasionally during cooking. Roast for 1 to 1¼ hours, basting occasionally.

Pork and Chili Balls ▶

HEAT 3–4

Serves 4

3 red poblano chilies

I garlic clove

4 tbsp olive or sunflower oil

2 tbsp orange juice

2 tsp honey, warmed

4 ham steaks, trimmed of excess fat

2 tbsp butter

⅔ cup dry white wine

⅔ cup chicken or vegetable stock

3-inch piece of cucumber, thinly peeled and cut into julienne strips

I tbsp cornstarch

I tbsp water

orange wedges and fresh herbs, to garnish

BRAISED HAM *with* CHILI SAUCE

Preheat the broiler.

Place the chilies in the broiler pan and broil for about 10 minutes, or until the skins have blistered and charred. Put into a plastic bag for 10 minutes before peeling and discarding the seeds.

Put the chilies into a food processor with the garlic, oil, orange juice and honey. Blend until smooth, then use to brush over both sides of the ham steaks. Leave in a cool place for at least 30 minutes.

Melt the butter in a large skillet and seal the steaks quickly on both sides. Add any remaining chili marinade, the wine and stock. Bring to a boil, then reduce the heat and simmer for 5 to 8 minutes, or until the steaks are cooked. Drain and place on warmed serving plates.

Add the cucumber to the pan, together with the cornstarch blended with the water. Cook, stirring occasionally, for 2 minutes, or until the sauce has thickened. Pour over the steaks and garnish with orange wedges and fresh herbs.

CHILI-BEEF BURGER

HEAT 5-6

Serves 4

2 oz fresh white bread, crusts removed

4 tbsp milk

1½ lb rump or chuck steak, trimmed
and ground

6 scallions, trimmed and finely
chopped

4 red Anaheim chilies, seeded and
finely chopped

1 tbsp freshly chopped oregano

salt and pepper

2 tbsp sunflower oil

2 onions, sliced

4 hamburger buns

Chili Mayonnaise (page 44)

½ small iceburg lettuce, shredded

2 large tomatoes, sliced

Chili Pepper Relish (page 47)

Soak the bread in the milk for 10 minutes, then drain and press out any excess liquid. Reserve.

Combine the beef with the soaked bread, scallions, 3 of the chilies, and the oregano with seasoning to taste. Mix together well. Slightly wet your hands and shape the mixture into 4 large burgers.

Heat the oil in a skillet and gently sauté the onions and remaining chili for 5 to 8 minutes until softened. Drain on paper towels and keep warm.

Preheat the broiler to medium-hot. Broil the burgers for 10 minutes, or until cooked to personal preference, turning at least once during cooking.

Split the buns and lightly toast under the broiler. Spread the bottoms with the Chili Mayonnaise and arrange some shredded lettuce on top. Place the cooked burgers on the lettuce and top with the cooked onions and chilies, sliced tomatoes and Chili Pepper Relish. Replace the bun tops and serve immediately.

BEEF RENDANG

HEAT 6-8

Serves 4

4 chipotle dried chilies, roasted,
rehydrated (page 16) and chopped

2 shallots, chopped

1 garlic clove, crushed

2 tbsp sunflower oil

1½ lb braising steak, trimmed and
cubed

1 tsp turmeric

2½ cups coconut milk

2 kaffir lime leaves

juice of 2 limes

salt and pepper

2 oz creamed coconut

freshly cooked rice, to serve

The dried chilies can be replaced with 3 or 4 red fresno chilies or 1 or 2 Thai (bird's eye) chilies. If a thickened sauce is preferred, add 1 to 1½ tbsp of flour when adding the turmeric. Check during cooking that the sauce is not becoming too thick; if it is, add a little more coconut milk or stock.

Make a paste with the chilies, shallots and garlic, and reserve.

Heat the oil in a large pan and sauté the beef in batches for 5 minutes, or until sealed. Remove from the pan with a slotted spoon and reserve.

Add the paste to the oil remaining in the pan and gently fry for 5 minutes. Add the beef and turmeric to the pan and cook for 2 minutes, stirring constantly.

Pour in the coconut milk and add the lime leaves, juice and seasoning. Bring to a boil, then cover the pan and reduce the heat. Simmer for 1½ hours, or until the meat is tender.

Add the creamed coconut gradually to the pan, stirring after each addition. Heat through for 5 minutes and serve with freshly cooked rice.

Serves 4

1¼ cups dry red wine

1 tbsp Worcestershire sauce

5 tbsp sunflower oil

4 red Scotch bonnet chilies, seeded
and sliced

1 tbsp roughly chopped fresh oregano

8 oz rump steak, trimmed and cut into
thin strips

1 red onion, cut into thin wedges

1 small red bell pepper, seeded and
cut into thin strips

1 small yellow bell pepper, seeded and
cut into thin strips

1 zucchini, trimmed and cut into thin
strips

8 to 12 wheat tortillas, lightly warmed,
sour cream, Salsa Verde (page 47)
and Guacamole (page 29), to serve

Serves 4

2 tbsp sunflower or groundnut oil

1-inch piece gingerroot, peeled
and grated

2 or 3 hontaka or Thai red chilies,
seeded and chopped

12 oz pork tenderloin, trimmed and
cut into thin strips

1 red bell pepper, seeded and cut into
strips

1 yellow bell pepper, seeded and cut
into strips

6 scallions, trimmed and sliced
diagonally

1 tbsp tomato paste

1 tbsp water

2 tsp soy sauce

1 tsp honey

1 tsp sesame oil

scallion tassel and flat-leafed parsley,
to garnish

BEEF FAJITAS

Fajitas are generally made from a poorer-quality cut of beef that has been marinated and then sliced across the grain and barbecued over a fierce heat. They should be served immediately, which is why many restaurants call this dish sizzling beef. For this recipe, a better quality of beef has been used but if you prefer, substitute chuck beef.

Mix the wine, Worcestershire sauce, 3 tbsp of the oil, 2 of the chilies and oregano together. Put the beef into a shallow dish and pour the wine marinade over. Cover and leave for at least 1 hour. Drain, reserving a little of the marinade.

Heat the remaining oil in a wok or large pan and quickly fry the remaining chilies and the vegetables for 3 to 5 minutes, or until crisp and slightly blackened on the edges. Remove from the pan and reserve.

Fry the beef in batches in the oil remaining in the pan for 2 to 3 minutes, or until sealed and browned and drain on paper towels. When all the meat has been browned, return the vegetables and 3 to 4 tbsp of the reserved marinade to the pan and heat through over a fierce heat, stirring frequently.

To serve, spread each warmed tortilla with sour cream, then place some of the beef mixture on top and add a spoonful of Salsa Verde. Roll up and eat with extra Salsa Verde and Guacamole.

SICHUAN HOT CHILI PORK

Sichuan cuisine is becoming increasingly popular in the West and there are many different variations on any Sichuan dish. Some err on the sweet side, but nearly all have a strong chili flavor.

Heat the oil in a wok or large pan and stir-fry the ginger and chilies for 2 minutes. Add the pork and stir-fry for a further 4 to 5 minutes. Then add the peppers and cook for 2 minutes.

Add the scallions and stir-fry for 30 seconds. Then add the tomato paste blended with the water, the soy sauce and honey. Stir-fry for 1 minute, then add the sesame oil and give one more stir. Serve immediately garnished with a scallion tassel and flat-leafed parsley.

Beef Fajitas ▶

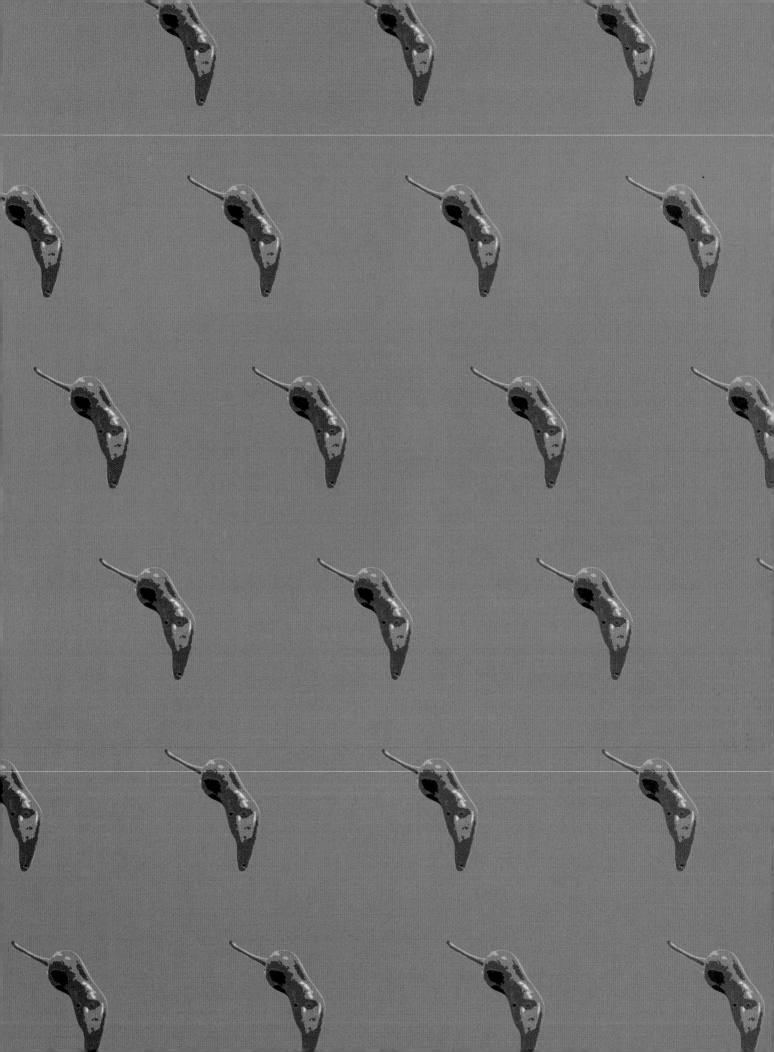

Chapter 8

Vegetarian

CHALUPAS

Tortillas

Serves 4

8 prepared wheat tortillas

Sauce
2 tsp sunflower oil
I small onion, chopped
2 red jalapeño chilies, seeded and
    chopped
14-oz can crushed tomatoes

Filling
½ small iceburg lettuce, shredded
I cup Frijoles Refritos (page 28)
½ cup grated hard cheese, such as
    Cheddar
4 scallions, trimmed and chopped
2 red jalapeño chilies, seeded and
    chopped
sour cream and lime wedges, to serve

Tortillas are the bases for many Mexican dishes such as enchilidas, burritos and empanadas. They are often filled with a variety of savory mixtures and almost always served with a side dish of refried beans. Here they are served crisp as filled tacos shells.

➤ Heat the oil in a small pan and gently sauté the onion and chilies for 5 minutes. Stir in the crushed tomatoes and bring to a boil. Reduce the heat and simmer for 15 minutes. Allow to cool slightly, then pass through a strainer to form a smooth purée. Cover and keep warm.

➤ Warm the tortillas slightly by placing in a nonstick skillet for about 30 seconds. Dampen the edges, then shape and pinch up the sides to form a boat shape.

➤ Fill the tortillas with the shredded lettuce and place the Frijoles Refritos on top. Spoon a little of the prepared sauce over. Divide the cheese between the tortillas and sprinkle over with the scallions and chopped chilies. Serve with sour cream and lime wedges.

CHILI PEPPER DAL

Serves 5

I tbsp sunflower oil
2 onions, sliced
2 garlic cloves, crushed
4 rocotillo chilies, seeded and chopped
I tsp turmeric
I cup green lentils
2½ cups water
salt and pepper
I red bell pepper, seeded, chopped
    and blanched
lightly fried onions and freshly chopped
    parsley, to garnish

Dal, or dhal, is a traditional Indian side dish or snack, and can be made from green or red lentils with assorted seasonings. Sometimes the mixture is formed into patties when served.

➤ Heat the oil and sauté the onion, garlic and chilies for 5 minutes. Stir in the turmeric and sauté for a further minute.

➤ Rinse and pick over the lentils if necessary; then add to the pan with the water and seasoning to taste. Bring to a boil. Cover

the pan, then reduce the heat and simmer for 35 minutes, or until cooked. (You may need to add a little extra water if the mixture is becoming too dry.)

➤ Stir the chopped, blanched red bell pepper into the dal for the last 10 minutes of cooking time. Adjust the seasoning and serve sprinkled with fried onions and parsley.

Chalupas ▶

HEAT 5

Serves 4

2 tbsp olive oil

1 large onion, chopped

1 small fennel bulb, trimmed and
   chopped

2 garlic cloves, crushed

4 red de agua chilies, seeded and
   sliced

8 sun-dried tomatoes

2 to 2½ cups vegetable stock

1½ cups grated carrot

1½ cups wiped and sliced oyster
   mushrooms

2 tbsp tomato paste

1 tsp sugar

salt and pepper

2 red bell peppers, seeded, blanched
   and cut into small strips

2 tbsp freshly chopped basil

10 to 12 oz fresh pasta, such as
   tagliatelle or rigatoni

shaved or freshly grated Parmesan
   cheese, to serve

freshly chopped basil, to garnish

PASTA *with* SPICY TOMATO SAUCE

Heat the oil in a pan and gently sauté the onion, fennel, garlic, chilies and sun-dried tomatoes for 3 minutes. Add ⅔ cup of the stock and simmer for 5 to 8 minutes.

Put into a food processor and blend to a chunky purée, adding extra stock if necessary. Return to the pan with all but 4 tbsp of the remaining stock.

Add the carrot, mushrooms, the tomato purée blended with the remaining stock, sugar and seasoning to taste. Bring to a boil, then simmer gently for 15 to 20 minutes, or until a thick consistency is formed. Add the bell peppers and chopped basil, and cook for a further 3 to 4 minutes.

Meanwhile, cook the pasta in boiling salted water for 4 to 6 minutes, or until al dente. Drain and return to the pan. Pour over the tomato sauce and toss well. Heat through for 2 to 3 minutes, stirring frequently. Garnish with freshly chopped basil and serve sprinkled with Parmesan.

HEAT 5

Serves 4

8 ready-made taco shells

1 tbsp sunflower oil

1 onion, thickly sliced

4 red de agua chilies, seeded and
   sliced

1 orange bell pepper, seeded and cut
   into thick strips

1 large zucchini, trimmed and cut into
   strips

1 heaped cup canned pinto beans,
   drained and rinsed

8½-oz can crushed tomatoes

½ small iceberg lettuce, shredded

2 ripe avocados, peeled, sliced and
   tossed in 3 tbsp lemon juice

1½ cups grated Cheddar cheese

Chili Mayonnaise (page 44),
   6 tbsp sour cream and canned
   chilies, to serve

SPICY VEGETABLE TACOS

Traditionally, a taco is a hand-held tortilla folded over the filling. The tortilla is warmed first so it folds easily. Now it is more usual to buy the ready-made taco shells. But don't forget to warm them first.

Preheat the oven to 350°F. Place the taco shells, open end down, on a baking sheet and heat for 2 to 3 minutes. Reserve.

Heat the oil in a pan and sauté the onion and chilies for 5 minutes. Add the orange bell pepper and zucchini, and cook for a further 3 minutes. Add the beans and tomatoes, and cook for 8 minutes, stirring frequently, or until a thick consistency is reached.

Fill the heated taco shells with the shredded lettuce and top with the chili and bean mixture. Place the sliced avocados on top and sprinkle with the grated cheese. Serve immediately with the Chili Mayonnaise, the sour cream and canned chilies.

Pasta with Spicy Tomato Sauce ▶

HEAT 8

Serves 4

6 oz instant dried noodles

2 tbsp sunflower oil

2 lemongrass stalks chopped, outer
leaves removed

1-inch piece gingerroot, peeled and
grated

1 red onion, cut into thin wedges

2 garlic cloves, crushed

4 red Thai chilies, seeded and sliced

1 red bell pepper, seeded and cut into
matchsticks

1 small carrot, very thinly sliced with a
vegetable peeler

1 small zucchini, trimmed and sliced
with a vegetable peeler

3 oz snow peas, trimmed and cut
diagonally in half

6 scallions, trimmed and diagonally
sliced

1 cup cashew nuts

2 tbsp soy sauce

juice of 1 orange

1 tsp honey

1 tbsp sesame oil

FRIED THAI NOODLES
with CHILLIES *and* VEGETABLES

*Rice or noodles, whether boiled or fried, form
the basis of most meals in Thailand. Thai
cooking is often pungent and hot but at the
same time is slightly perfumed. This is often
due to the lemongrass which features strongly
in most of their dishes.*

Cook the noodles in lightly salted boiling
water for 3 minutes. Drain, plunge into cold
water, then drain again and reserve.

Heat the oil in a wok or large pan and
stir-fry the lemongrass and ginger for
2 minutes. Discard the lemongrass and
ginger, keeping the oil in the pan.

Add the onion, garlic and chilies and
stir-fry for 2 minutes. Add the red bell pepper
and cook for a further 2 minutes. Add the
remaining vegetables and stir-fry for 2 minutes.
Then add the reserved noodles and cashew
nuts with the soy sauce, orange juice and
honey. Stir-fry for 1 minute. Add the sesame
oil and stir-fry for 30 seconds. Serve
immediately.

HEAT 6–7

Serves 4

2 tbsp sunflower oil

1 large onion, sliced

2 garlic cloves, crushed

4 Kenyan or green fresno chilies,
seeded and sliced

1 tsp ground coriander

1 tsp ground cumin

5 cloves, ground

8 green cardamom pods

1 tsp turmeric

1 tsp fenugreek seeds, lightly bruised

2 cups vegetable stock

1 lb okra, trimmed

⅔ cup canned pinto or kidney beans,
drained and rinsed

4 tbsp plain yogurt

2 tbsp freshly chopped cilantro

2 tbsp flaked almonds, toasted

OKRA *and* BEAN CURRY

Heat the oil in a pan and sauté the onion,
garlic and chilies for 5 minutes. Add the spices
and sauté for a further 3 minutes. Stir in the
stock and bring to a boil. Cover the pan,
reduce the heat and simmer for 10 minutes.

Prick the okra a few times with a fork and
add to the pan with the beans. Cook gently for
8 to 10 minutes, or until the okra is tender. Stir
in the yogurt and cilantro, and heat through
for a further minute. Serve sprinkled with
the almonds.

◀ *Fried Thai Noodles with
Chilies and Vegetables*

CHILIES *in* NUT SAUCE

Chillis en nogado

HEAT 2–3

Serves 4

8 red poblano or red New
Mexico chilies
2 tbsp butter
1½ cups peeled, seeded and sliced ripe
tomatoes
juice of 2 limes
2 firm, almost ripe avocados, peeled
and seeds removed
salad leaves, to serve

Sauce
½ cup pecan or walnuts
2 tbsp blanched almonds
⅔ cup crème fraîche
1 tsp honey
2 tbsp grated Parmesan cheese

Traditionally, this dish is green, white and red, the colors of the Mexican flag. Ideally green walnuts are used for the sauce but if these are unavailable, ripe walnuts can be substituted.

🌶 Finely grind the nuts for the sauce in a food processor. Combine with the crème fraîche and honey. Put into a small saucepan and stir in the cheese. Heat through gently, stirring frequently.
🌶 Preheat the broiler.
🌶 Place the chilies in the broiler pan and broil for 10 minutes until the skins have blistered and started to blacken. Remove from the heat and put into a plastic bag. Leave for 10 minutes. Skin the chilies and discard the seeds and membranes. Cut into strips.
🌶 Melt the butter in a pan and sauté the chilies for 5 minutes. Add the chopped tomatoes and lime juice, and sauté for a further 3 minutes. Slice the avocados, add to the pan and heat through for 5 minutes, stirring occasionally.
🌶 Serve on a bed of salad leaves with the nut sauce.

VEGETARIAN ENCHILADAS

HEAT 5

Serves 4

2 tbsp sunflower oil
1 large onion, thinly sliced
2 garlic cloves, crushed
4 green de agua chilies, seeded and
sliced
2¼ cups peeled, seeded and chopped
ripe tomatoes
1 tbsp tomato paste
1 tbsp water
2 zucchini, trimmed and cut into
matchsticks
1½ cups grated cheese, such as
Cheddar
6 scallions, trimmed and chopped
8 wheat tortillas
fresh herbs, to garnish
Chili Pepper Relish (page 47), to serve

Most people associate Mexican food with snacks such as tacos or enchiladas, which the Mexicans call antojitos, *meaning little whim or craving. They nearly all consist of a tortilla presented in a variety of ways and can be found at roadside cafes, market places and stalls to be eaten at any time of the day.*

🌶 Preheat the oven to 400°F.
🌶 Heat the oil in a skillet and gently sauté the onion, garlic and chilies for 5 minutes. Add the tomatoes and the tomato paste blended with the water and bring to a boil. Cover the pan, reduce the heat and simmer for 15 minutes.

Add the zucchini, 1 cup of the cheese and the scallions, and stir well.
🌶 Divide the filling between the tortillas and fold into quarters. Place in a shallow baking dish and sprinkle with the remaining cheese. Bake for 15 minutes, or until the cheese is bubbly. Garnish with herbs and serve immediately with Chili Pepper Relish.

Vegetarian Enchiladas ▶

BRAISED OKRA
with CHILIES

HEAT 5

Serves 4

1 lb okra

2 tbsp sunflower oil

1 large onion, thinly sliced

4 green Anaheim chilies, seeded and sliced

1 green bell pepper, seeded and sliced

1½ cups peeled, seeded and chopped tomatoes

salt and pepper

3 tbsp water

plain yogurt, to serve

Trim the okra and prick a few times with a fork.

Heat the oil in a pan and sauté the onion and chilies for 5 minutes, or until softened. Add the green bell pepper and cook for a further 2 minutes.

Stir in the chopped tomatoes, the okra and water with seasoning to taste and bring to a boil. Reduce the heat, cover the pan and simmer for 8 minutes, or until the okra is tender. Serve immediately topped with spoonfuls of yogurt.

Braised Okra with Chilies and above, ▶
Potatoes with Chili, Peanuts and Cheese

SPICY PEPPER PIZZA

HEAT 5–6

Serves 4

1 tbsp sunflower oil

1 onion, chopped

2 garlic cloves, crushed

5 red jalapeño chilies, seeded and
thinly sliced

14 oz-can crushed tomatoes

2 tbsp tomato paste

2 tbsp freshly chopped oregano

2 tsp ground cumin

2 prepared 8-inch pizza bases

2 red bell peppers, skinned and
seeded

2 green bell peppers, skinned and
seeded

2 yellow bell peppers, skinned and
seeded

1½ cups grated mozzarella cheese

⅓ cup pitted black olives

Preheat the oven to 400°F. Lightly oil 2 baking sheets.

Heat the oil in a pan and sauté the onion, garlic and chilies for 5 minutes. Add the crushed tomatoes, tomato paste, oregano and cumin, and bring to a boil. Reduce the heat and simmer for 10 to 15 minutes, or until a thick sauce consistency is reached.

Spread the sauce over the pizza bases. Slice the peppers and arrange on top of the sauce. Cover with the cheese and arrange the olives on top. Bake for 25 minutes, or until the cheese is golden and bubbly.

HEAT 4–5

Serves 4

Sauce

1½ cups peeled, seeded and chopped
    green tomatoes

3 shallots, finely chopped

2 or 3 garlic cloves, crushed

3 green jalapeño chilies, seeded and
    chopped

⅔ cup vegetable stock

I tsp honey

2 tsp arrowroot

I tbsp water

2 tbsp freshly chopped flat-leafed
    parsley

Turnovers

2 cups grated Cheddar cheese

6 scallions, trimmed and chopped

⅓ cup pine nuts, toasted

6 dried chipotle chilies, roasted and
    rehydrated (page 16)

2 tbsp butter

4 cups wiped and sliced mushrooms

8 prepared wheat tortillas

I medium egg, beaten

oil for deep-frying

salad leaves, to serve

CHEESE TURNOVERS
with GREEN TOMATO SAUCE

Enchiladas with Salsa Verde

Enchiladas were first made by Native Americans. In the northern state of Sonora they developed a white flour tortilla after the Spanish had introduced wheat to the region. These are usually larger than corn tortillas and they too are often used for making burritos.

❧ Make the sauce. Put the green tomatoes, shallots, garlic and chilies into a saucepan and simmer for 5 to 7 minutes, or until softened. Then put into a food processor with the stock and honey and blend to a purée. Pass through a fine strainer.

❧ Return to the pan and simmer for 5 minutes. Blend the arrowroot with the water and stir into the sauce. Cook, stirring constantly until the sauce thickens and clears. If not to be used immediately, thicken when required and store, covered, in the refrigerator.

❧ Mix the cheese, scallions and pine nuts together. Discard the seeds from the rehydrated chilies and chop the flesh. Add to the cheese mixture and mix together well. Reserve.

❧ Melt the butter in a small pan and sauté the mushrooms for 3 minutes. Drain.

❧ Place a spoonful of the cheese mixture on top of each tortilla and top with a spoonful of the mushrooms. Brush the edges of each tortilla with a little beaten egg, then fold over to form a crescent shape and pinch the edges together firmly. Brush the edges lightly with the beaten egg and fold the edges over again to give a rope effect and a more secure seal.

❧ Heat the oil to 350°F and fry the turnovers in batches for 2 to 3 minutes, or until golden. Drain on paper towels and serve on a bed of salad leaves, and the green sauce.

HEAT 2–3

Serves 4

8 fresh banana or other large chilies
    about 6 inches long

I tsp chili powder

I cup prepared Frijoles Refritos
    (page 28)

3 tbsp all-purpose flour

3 large eggs, separated

oil for deep-frying

I fresh red Anaheim chili, seeded and
    sliced

2 tbsp freshly chopped flat-leafed
    parsley

grated lime peel

Salsa Verde (page 47), to serve

STUFFED CHILIES *with* BEANS

Chili rellenos de frijoles

❧ Preheat the broiler to high. Place the chilies in the broiler pan and broil until the skins blister and begin to blacken. Remove from the heat and put into a plastic bag. Leave for about 10 minute to allow the chilies to sweat, then carefully discard the skins. Make a slit down the center lengthwise and discard the seeds and membrane. Sprinkle with chili powder.

❧ Stuff the chilies with the Frijoles Refritos and overlap the edges to encase the filling.

❧ Sift a scant 2 tbsp of the flour into a bowl, then add the egg yolks and beat well to form a

smooth consistency. Whisk the egg whites until stiff and standing in peaks, then carefully fold into the egg yolk mixture.

❧ Pour the oil into a pan to a depth of about 2 inches and heat to 350°F.

❧ Coat the stuffed chilies in the remaining flour and dip into the batter. Fry in the hot oil for 3 to 4 minutes, or until golden brown. Drain on paper towels, then arrange on a serving plate and sprinkle with the sliced chilies, herbs and lime peel. Serve with Salsa Verde.

Enchiladas with Salsa Verde ▶

CAULIFLOWER
and TOMATO CURRY

Gobbi tamatar

HEAT 5

Serves 4

3 cups cauliflower flowerets

1½ cups diced potatoes

2 tbsp sunflower oil

2-inch piece gingerroot, peeled and
  grated

1 onion, sliced

2 garlic cloves, crushed

5 dried ancho chilies, roasted and
  rehydrated (page 16)

1 tsp coriander seeds

1 tsp cumin seeds

1 tsp fenugreek seeds

1 tsp turmeric

2 tbsp tomato paste

2 tbsp water

3 cups peeled, seeded and chopped
  tomatoes

⅔ cup coconut milk

⅔ cup plain yogurt

fresh flat-leafed parsley or cilantro,
  to garnish

naan bread, freshly cooked rice,
  poppadoms and chutneys,
  to serve

*If dried chilies are unavailable, use 3 or 4
green fresno chilies or 1 to 1½ tsp medium-hot
chili powder.*

🌶 Cook the cauliflower in lightly salted
boiling water for 3 minutes, drain and reserve

🌶 Cook the potatoes in lightly salted boiling
water for 10 minutes, or until just tender.
Drain and reserve.

🌶 Heat the oil in a large pan and gently sauté
the ginger for 3 minutes, then discard the
ginger. Add the onion, garlic and chopped
rehydrated chilies, and sauté for 3 minutes.
Add the spices and cook, stirring frequently,
for 3 minutes.

🌶 Blend the tomato paste with the water and
add to the pan with the tomatoes and coconut
milk. Bring to just below boiling point and
simmer for 5 minutes. Add the reserved
cauliflower and potatoes, and cook for a
further 5 to 8 minutes, or until the vegetables
are just tender.

🌶 Stir in the yogurt and heat through for
2 minutes. Garnish with fresh herbs and serve
with warm naan bread and rice, poppadoms
and chutneys.

SAG ALOO SAMOSAS

Serves 4

3 tbsp sunflower oil

I onion, chopped

3 green fresno chilies, seeded and
   chopped

I tsp ground cumin

I tsp ground coriander

¾ cup diced potatoes, cooked

¾ cup diced carrots, cooked

I2 oz spinach, cooked and chopped

4 large sheets filo pastry dough

oil for deep-frying

green salad, naan and assorted
   chutneys, to serve

Samosas are a typical Indian snack with every region having its own particular filling. It takes a little practice to achieve a good shape, but once you have mastered the art you will be surprised how easy they are, in fact, to prepare.

◥ Heat the sunflower oil in a pan and sauté the onion and chilies for 3 minutes. Add the spices and sauté for a further 3 minutes. Then add the cooked vegetables and mix well together. Allow to cool.

◥ Cut the filo pastry dough into 10 x 4-inch strips. Place 2 tbsp of the filling at one end of each strip and fold the dough over diagonally to form a triangle. Continue folding triangles along the strip, brushing the edges with a little water.

◥ Heat the oil for deep frying to 350°F and fry the samosas in batches for about 5 minutes, or until golden. Drain on paper towels and serve with green salad, naan and assorted chutneys.

ACAR ACAR

Indonesian mixed vegetables

Serves 4

4 Thai red chilies

I large onion, chopped

3 garlic cloves

8 oz fresh peanuts, shelled and
   roasted

3 tbsp sunflower oil

3 tbsp granulated sugar

2½ cups white-wine vinegar

8 oz green beans

I cucumber

2 red bell peppers, seeded

I½ cups cauliflower flowerets

I fresh pineapple, flesh removed
   from shell, cored and diced

salt and pepper

a few threads of saffron or
   ½ tsp turmeric

A Malaysian pickle similar to British piccalilli. Often served with curries or cold meat or even fish dishes.

◥ Put the chilies, onion and garlic into a food processor and blend until smooth. Reserve. Grind or process the peanuts until lightly chopped and reserve.

◥ Heat the oil in a large pan and gently sauté the chili purée for 4 minutes. Add the sugar and vinegar, bring to a boil, then simmer for 5 minutes.

◥ Add the peanut paste and then the vegetables and pineapple with the seasoning and saffron or turmeric. Simmer for 2 minutes, stirring constantly. If serving hot, heat through gently for 4 to 5 minutes, stirring frequently. If serving cold, heat through for 2 minutes, then place in a serving dish, cover and chill. Stir thoroughly before serving.

◥ If stored in sealed screw-top glass jars, Acar Acar may be kept in the refrigerator or a cool place for up to 1 month.

SPICED EGGPLANT PURÉE

HEAT 5

Serves 6

2 large eggplants, about 1 lb in weight

4 red Anaheim chilies

4 garlic cloves

grated peel and juice of 1 large lemon

1 tsp ground cumin

1 tsp ground coriander

1 tsp ground cinnamon

¾ cup cream cheese

cumin seeds, to garnish

pita breads and crudités, to serve

Preheat the oven to 400°F.

Rinse the eggplants and prick a few times. Place in the oven directly on an oven shelf and bake for 40 minutes, or until very soft and the eggplants have begun to collapse. Place the chilies and garlic on a baking sheet and place on another shelf. Cook the chilies and garlic for about 10 minutes, or until the skins have begun to wrinkle. Remove from the oven and put into a plastic bag for 10 minutes. Peel and discard the seeds from the chilies and the skins from the garlic, and reserve.

Allow the eggplants to cool, then strip off the skin and put the flesh into a food processor with the chilies, garlic, lemon rind and juice, and the spices. Blend to form a smooth purée, then add the cream cheese and blend again. Transfer to a serving bowl and fork the top.

Chill for at least 30 minutes. Garnish with cumin seeds and serve with pita breads and crudités.

INDEX